Women Writers

General Editors: *Eva Figes* and *Adele King*

Published titles

Margaret Atwood, Barbara Hill Rigney
Jane Austen, Meenakshi Mukherjee
Elizabeth Bowen, Phyllis Lassner
Anne Brontë, Elizabeth Langland
Charlotte Brontë, Pauline Nestor
Emily Brontë, Lyn Pykett
Fanny Burney, Judy Simons
Willa Cather, Susie Thomas
Colette, Diana Holmes
Ivy Compton-Burnett, Kathy Justice Gentile
Emily Dickinson, Joan Kirkby
George Eliot, Kristin Brady
Sylvia Plath, Susan Bassnett
Christina Stead, Diana Brydon
Eudora Welty, Louise Westling
Edith Wharton, Katherine Joslin

Forthcoming

Elizabeth Barrett Browning, Marjorie Stone
Mrs Gaskell, Jane Spencer
Doris Lessing, Margaret Moan Rowe
Katherine Mansfield, Diane DeBell
Toni Morrison, Nellie McKay
Jean Rhys, Carol Rumens
Christina Rossetti, Linda Marshall
Stevie Smith, Romana Huk
Muriel Spark, Judith Sproxton
Gertrude Stein, Jane Bowers
Virginia Woolf, Clare Hanson

Women Writers

George Eliot

Kristin Brady

MACMILLAN

First published 1992 by
MACMILLAN EDUCATION LTD
Houndmills, Basingstoke, Hampshire RG21 2XS
and London
Companies and representatives
throughout the world

ISBN 0–333–43286–X hardcover
ISBN 0–333–43287–8 paperback

A catalogue record for this book is available
from the British Library.

Typeset by Footnote Graphics, Warminster, Wiltshire
Printed in Hong Kong

Contents

Acknowledgements

In writing this book, I have profited from conversations with many colleagues, friends and students, but I would like to give special mention to Professor Elizabeth D. Harvey, for her many insights on feminist theory; to Dr Judith Williams, for her astute editorial eye; and to Elisabeth MacDonald, for her tireless footwork in the library. My particular thanks also go to Professor Richard Hillman, whose professional advice, emotional support and culinary genius sustained me at every point.

A longer version of the section on *Romola* appeared as 'Gender and History in George Eliot's *Romola*' in the *Dalhousie Review* (67 [1987]: 257–74); I am grateful to the editor for permission to reprint it.

Editors' Preface

The study of women's writing has been long neglected by a male critical establishment both in academic circles and beyond. As a result, many women writers have either been unfairly neglected or have been marginalised in some way, so that their true influence and importance has been ignored. Other women writers have been accepted by male critics and academics, but on terms which seem, to many women readers of this generation, to be false or simplistic. In the past the internal conflicts involved in being a woman in a male-dominated society have been largely ignored by readers of both sexes, and this has affected our reading of women's work. The time has come for a serious reassessment of women's writing in the light of what we understand today.

This series is designed to help in that reassessment.

All the books are written by women because we believe that men's understanding of feminist critique is only, at best, partial. And besides, men have held the floor quite long enough.

EVA FIGES
ADELE KING

For Richard

1 Constructing the Man-Woman: George Eliot as Icon

Somewhat to my surprise, I found her intensely feminine. Her slight figure, – it might almost be called diminutive, – her gentle, persuasive air, her constrained gesticulation, the low, sweet voice, – all were as far removed from the repulsive phenomenon, the 'man-woman,' as it is possible to conceive. The brow alone seemed to betray her intellectual superiority.[1]

The life and reputation of Marian Evans, the woman who published under the masculine pseudonym 'George Eliot', provide an unusual case study for the feminist critic. Unlike most women writing and publishing during the nineteenth century, Eliot enjoyed a position of high intellectual prominence during her lifetime and has continued to occupy an eminent place in the canon of English literature. There is no need to unearth her works from the long-buried tradition of women's writing or to insist that they be treated seriously. This does not mean, however, that there is no place for feminist re-readings of Eliot's life and works. That she was one of the few women of her time to achieve major literary status makes her, in fact, a valuable focus for exploring the contradictions that emerge when a woman in a patriarchal society successfully appropriates the 'masculine' position of the writer: though Eliot was never denied a niche in the predominantly male literary canon, she has always been given a special status within it, as a writer whose accomplishments were extraordinary *for a woman*; no male writer has been analysed in terms of gender to the extent that George Eliot has been. Before describing Eliot's life, therefore, I intend first to examine the critical discourse that has interpreted her during the century or so since her death – a discourse that has established a virtual iconography of Eliot as a pathological monster created by the unnatural conjunction of a masculine mind with a feminine body.

The icon of Eliot as that 'repulsive phenomenon, the "man-woman"', emerged from a nineteenth-century equation of woman with her reproductive organs that was based on a scientific model of incommensurable sexual difference. Such a definition, which admitted no commonality between genders, naturalised – and thus justified – the already existing social and cultural differences between the sexes. If woman was the heart (that is to say, uterus) in relation to the man's head (that is to say, brain), then the separate spheres of the man's public world and the woman's domestic world were merely social manifestations of essential, natural differences. To unsettle these binary oppositions was to tamper with nature itself.

An influential idea in this construction of incommensurable difference between the sexes was that of the human body as a closed system containing a limited amount of heat or energy. The woman's body, it was believed – not only by the bearing and nurturing of children, but even by the periodic function of menstruation – expended physical heat through the reproductive organs, leaving little or no energy that could travel to the head or brain. The male body, however – free of the draining properties of the uterus – expended energy in a mental direction. Associated with woman, moreover, was the whole range of behaviour labelled by nineteenth-century scientific and medical discourse as hysteria: to possess a uterus was to have an excess of nervous energy which, when given too much expression, had to be contained by such measures as the rest-cure (which included systematic douching), clitoridectomy and institutionalisation – not to mention marriage. For this reason, the female body was perceived to be not merely different from the male body but also the source of a distinct pathology. The nineteenth century thus inscribed on its construction of woman a host of anxieties about the body and, more particularly, about sexuality.

It was in this climate of thinking that George Eliot's character, life and writing were first constructed by her contemporaries, who attempted, in various ways, to define her according to their own preconceived notions about gender difference. This task was a monumentally difficult one, however, for Marian Evans failed in significant ways to conform to the cultural imperatives. A woman who was considered to be unattractive to men and who openly expressed her sexuality in a relationship outside marriage while never bearing children; a woman who usurped the masculine prerogatives of learning the classical languages, of mastering current scientific and philosophical ideas, and of supporting herself as a writer; a woman who readily assumed the position of sage among her friends and associates – such a woman both invited and resisted the standard reduction to a hysterical uterus. Thus, though the extant responses to Eliot by no means represent a monolithic reaction, many of them can be classified in one of two general categories. The tendency was either to insist on Eliot's essential feminity or to see her as a freak of nature, a monstrous anomaly in whom feminine and masculine traits waged a destructive conflict. In both these cases, moreover, there was a general preoccupation with Eliot's female body, the site of her potentially hysterical uterus and the sign of her problematic position in the symbolic order.

Among Eliot's contemporaries, there was often an interest in Eliot's head – the assumption being that she was born with a male head and a female trunk. These interpretations were often shaped by the influential pseudoscience of

phrenology, which, though it did not concern itself explicitly with gender difference, implied a theory of female
inferiority by its assumption that large brains were more
intelligent than small ones. For those adhering to such
thinking, Eliot's appearance was perplexing, and many
people commented on what they perceived to be the unusually large size of her head and features. Annie Adams
Fields, for example, speculated that 'her brain must be
heavier than most men's',[2] and both Alfred Tennyson and
Charles Eliot Norton commented on Eliot's 'masculine
face'. Even as recently as 1955, Humphry House noted,
without offering a source, that Eliot's skull 'was said to be
broader from brow to ear than any other recorded skull
except Napoleon's'.[3]

Speculations about the size of Eliot's head often led to
theories about its relation to her female body. Joseph Jacobs
remarked on 'the massiveness of the head as contrasted with
the frailty of the body', while Kegan Paul described what he
saw as a 'disproportion' between Eliot's 'grand and massive'
head and the 'little fragile' body that had to bear 'this weight
of brow and brain' – a phenomenon that George Willis
Cooke in his 1883 biography took as an explanation for
Eliot's weak health.[4] Predictably, observations about the
size of Eliot's head led to speculations about what happened
inside it. Herbert Spencer, for example, though he admitted
that she had 'high philosophical capacity with extensive
acquisition', found her 'abnormal' mental powers to involve
'a physiological cost which the feminine organization will
not bear without injury more or less profound'.[5]

While Spencer fantasised about the harm that a powerful
philosophical mind could do to a weak female body, another
old friend of Eliot's turned his attention to the consequences
for Eliot's writings of her being a woman. Frederic Harrison
took the natural image of giving birth, often used to describe
the creative work of both female and male writers, and –
transforming the image from the biological to the pathological

– made writing seem a grotesquely unnatural activity for a middle-aged woman and hence the occasion for a 'dangerous crisis'. Harrison also transformed the image of '[p]arturition . . . late in the mother's life' into still another metaphor for creativity that implied the inappropriateness of Eliot's body for her mental task. Eliot's 'powerful mind', he suggested, possessed the 'rich gifts' of a male artist like Beethoven, but her books gave a 'sense of almost painful elaboration' because she produced them as if 'with an unfamiliar and uncongenial instrument, . . . an untuned and dilapidated old piano'.[6] If George Eliot's mind was a burden to her body, as Spencer thought, then her body, in Harrison's view, was a grossly inadequate 'instrument' for that mind. In both cases, the female metabolism was seen as a handicap for the professional thinker and writer.

Gendered readings of the sort that Spencer's and Harrison's appraisals represent are not confined to the observations of a few of Eliot's perplexed intimate friends. From the time that she first became established as a writer, and throughout the biography and criticism about her – even in remarks that are meant to praise – there is a long tradition of dissecting Eliot's body and mind according to their presumed feminine and masculine traits. After meeting Eliot in 1873, for example, John Fiske wrote to his wife that there was 'nothing a bit masculine about her; she is thoroughly feminine and looks and acts as if she were made for nothing but to mother babies. But she has a power of *stating* an argument equal to any man' (*GEL* 5: 464). In a similar vein of admiration and bafflement, Bret Harte wrote in 1880, 'She reminds you continually of a man – a bright, gentle, lovable, philosophical man – without being a bit *masculine*'.[7] Both Fiske and Harte, like many others, seem to have been fearful of applying the label 'masculine' to George Eliot, even though they could see attributes in her that they thought were exclusively confined to men. To do so, apparently, would be to deny her femininity and therefore to identify her with the stereotypical blue-stocking, who, as Elaine Showalter has noted, 'was seen as tough, aggressive, pedantic, vain, and ugly'.[8] There was simply no acceptable place in the sexual iconography of Victorian partiarchy for the intellectual woman.

A letter Henry James wrote to his father when he first met Eliot in 1869 typifies those accounts by men (and women) who had difficulty in reconciling her physical appearance and personality with their own assumptions about gender difference. James declared Eliot to be 'magnificently ugly' and 'deliciously hideous', but found himself to be 'literally in love with this great horse-faced blue-stocking'. His account reads like a jumbled list of the binary oppositions that define sexual difference in partiarchal culture: references to Eliot's 'beauty' and 'charm', to her 'delightful expression' and 'soft' voice, to her 'sweetness', 'simpleness' and 'shyness' evoke a conventional image of femininity, while allusions to 'ugliness', potency, 'sagacity', 'knowledge, pride and power', to 'consciousness', 'frankness', and 'remote indifference' signal stereotypical masculinity. In order to contain all these seemingly conflicting traits, James attributed to Eliot a 'larger circumference' than that of any woman he had ever seen – thus giving her a width that could encompass in one body what culture had divided between two.[9]

What the youthful James described in such ambivalently enthusiastic terms made George Eliot for any others a uniformly troubling and forbidding presence. In the eyes of some later writers – among them, George Bernard Shaw and W.B. Yeats – this 'larger circumference' often transformed her, as Showalter has suggested, into a phallic mother whose massive authority intimidated future generations.[10] A common response to the magnitude of Eliot's influence was to strip it of its power by ridiculing it. Algernon Swinburne, for example, called Eliot 'an Amazon thrown sprawling over the crupper of her spavined and spur-galled Pegasus'[11] – a mock epic image deriding not only Eliot's body and her art but also, more particularly, the relationship between the two.

A mocking strategy seems also to colour the somewhat milder observations of William Barry, writing in 1904, who in commenting on 'a certain affinity of [Eliot's] mind with the masculine', declared that 'Goethe has often been called the Poet of Science; George Eliot perhaps deserves the name of the Epic Pythoness of Science'.[12] Here the reverent and neutrally intellectual term 'Poet', applied to the male writer Goethe, becomes, when applied to the female writer, 'Pythoness', a reference to the Greek oracle. By associating Eliot with the priestess whose voice served as a medium of prophecy in the temple of Apollo, Barry thus implicitly defines her writing, not as the articulate and coherent discourse of the male poet – who, like Apollo, speaks clearly – but as the contamination of that discourse by the female oracle, whose voice makes Apollo's message inscrutable. To call Eliot a pythoness rather than a poet is thus not merely to acknowledge her gender; it is simultaneously a way of gendering her discourse – and so of excluding its presumably occult qualities from the pure category of masculine poetry. The strategy also provides a way of making Eliot the *medium* of a discourse rather than its orginator. More generally, the pythoness reference suggests a sinister physical power and, when compared to the term 'poet', a transformation not simply from the poetic to the oracular and from the reverent to the sinister, but also from the human to the bestial: the woman poet is made more animal than human, more physical than mental – and, as such, more ridiculous than sublime. She is made, in short, hysterical. As a 'Pythoness', she is also, paradoxically, a female phallus – an icon of feminine knowledge and potency.

A similarly mixed iconography informs the comments of Edmund Gosse, who in 1906 called George Eliot a 'ludicrous pythoness' and in 1919 reminisced concerning her

physical appearance – about which he confessed to having a
'violent interest' – as that of

> a large, thick-set sybil, dreamy and immobile, whose
> massive features, somewhat grim when seen in profile,
> were incongruously bordered by a hat, always in the
> height of the Paris fashion, which in those days com-
> monly included an immense ostrich feather. . . . The con-
> trast between the solemnity of the face and the frivolity
> of the head-gear had something pathetic and provincial
> about it.[13]

Gazing at Eliot's head from the perspective of an urban
male, Gosse could make her look ridiculous (and himself
superior) by mocking her transgressing of two carefully
guarded boundaries: class and gender. He therefore singled
out Eliot's incongruous 'head-gear' – her attempt to disguise her provincial roots by wearing high fashion, as well as
her feminine covering for what was so often viewed as a
masculine brain. The sibyl image, another reference to an
oracle, adds to the sense of incongruity, for when visualised
as wearing a large feather the prophetess appears absurd and
her knowledge loses its potent danger. Again the oracle –
even as she achieves masculine recognition – is ridiculed for
her body and thus deprived of her mysterious influence.
Gosse indirectly attacks Eliot's literary status by lampoon-
ing her body.

A similar linking of Eliot's literary reputation with her
physical appearance characterises David Cecil's reference,
made in 1934, to Eliot as standing 'at the gateway between
the old novel and the new, a massive caryatid, heavy of
countenance, uneasy of attitude'. Cecil's remarks bring
together two dimensions of the caryatid image: like the
priestesses in the temple of Diana at Carthage, Eliot is the
guardian of secret female knowledge; and even more than
the draped female figures standing as pillars in Greek archi-

tecture (more phallic mothers?), Eliot is 'massive' and
'heavy'. Though Cecil ends his remarks by admitting that
Eliot was none the less 'noble, monumental, profoundly
impressive' (*Century* 210), the literalising of her into a large
and immobile statue, a 'massive' and overwhelming physical presence, is common to both his censure and his praise.
The emphasis on heaviness, like Gosse's on incongruity,
undermines any suggestion that Eliot had real power in her
role as prophetess.

An oppressive sense of Eliot's physical control seems also
to inform Cecil's comparison of Eliot to a school-teacher,

> kindly but just, calm but censorious, with birchrod in
> hand to use as she thinks right, and lists of good and bad
> conduct marks pinned neatly to her desk. And when we
> see all the vivid disorderly vitality of human nature
> ranged before her for carefully measured approval or
> condemnation, we tend to feel rebellious and resentful.
> (*Century* 206)

Here Cecil associates himself with that 'vivid disorderly
vitality' suppressed by the phallic mother, her birchrod in
hand. In a comically rendered reversal of the standard power
relations between the sexes within partriarchy, he assaults
Eliot's literary reputation by invoking an image of feminine
tyranny and identifying with her victims.

The defensive humour of Gosse's and Cecil's comments –
with their reduction of Eliot to a physical body and their
iconography of femininity as occult, absurd, monumental
and tyrannical – appears to mask a profound fear. If a
woman is appropriating the male position, they seem implicitly to be asking, how and where is the masculine to be
constructed? And what is the relationship of the male reader
and writer to a female figure who has upset the binary
opposition that places the masculine above the feminine? As
Mary Jacobus has described such a situation, 'Faced with

sexual differences, the man sees [femininity] as unfriendly
to his own narcissistically conceived identity; femininity is
dangerous because, by "infecting" him, it might erase the
distinction which buttresses his idea of masculinity.' As
Jacobus sees it, this sense of the feminine as a threat to
masculinity is the expression of a fear, not only of gender difference, but also of the *différance* that informs textuality itself:

> Women become a metaphor for the singleness that writ-
> ing itself has lost, so that the woman writer comes to
> figure both for herself and for her readers the hysterical
> doubleness and incompleteness which representation
> must repress in order to figure as true, unified, and whole
> – as masculine, or bearing 'the serious stamp of
> science'.[14]

Significantly, many of the gendered criticisms of Eliot's
writing ascribe to her a feminine lack of exactly those illu-
sive characteristics of truth and wholeness that repress *différance* in the literary text. The young Henry James, who
could declare himself in love with the potent beauty of
Eliot's physical presence, reviewed her early novels with a
profound sense of masculine superiority. Praising Eliot for
having 'a certain masculine comprehensiveness that [Maria
Edgeworth and Jane Austen] lack', he went on to say that
she remained 'a delightfully feminine writer' because she
had 'the microscopic observation, not a myriad of whose
keen notations are worth a single one of those great syn-
thetic guesses with which a real master attacks the truth'
(*Century* 42). As is so often the case, praise for a presumably
feminine gift simultaneously occasions an assertion of lack.
By definition, feminine multiplicity is made inferior to masculine phallocentric unity: difference and *différance* must be
suppressed.

The same hierarchical thinking informs George Saintsbury's remarks, made in 1895, that Eliot possessed 'in no

ordinary degree the female faculty of receiving, assimilating, and reproducing', but that she lacked 'in any great degree the male faculties of creation and judgment' (*Century* 166). Feminine writing was seen as passive and imitative, in other words, while masculine writing was presented as active and 'creative'. A different distinction was made by John Morley, who attributed Eliot's 'ever-deepening sense of the pain of the world' to feminine weakness. 'She could not, he commented, as virile natures should, reconcile herself to nature.'[15] In the same vein, Leslie Stephen regretted the 'want of masculine fibre in George Eliot', [16] and Arnold Bennett summarised the feeling of many of his generation:

> Her style, though not without shrewdness, is too rank to have any enduring vitality. People call it 'masculine.' Quite wrong! It is downright, aggressive, sometimes rude, but genuinely masculine, never. On the contrary it is transparently feminine – feminine in its lack of restraint, its wordiness, and the utter absence of feeling for form which characterizes it. The average woman italicizes freely. George Eliot, of course, had trained herself too well to do that, at least formally; yet her constant, undue insistence springs from the same essential weakness, and amounts practically to the same expedient. (*Century* 169)

Here Bennett presents Eliot as exceptional among women writers chiefly because she could disguise herself as a man, but congratulates himself for seeing through her superior self-cultivation and shrewdness, finding underneath them her essentially feminine weakness. Again, the mental and the literary are reduced, when seen in the context of a woman, to the physical: it is the feminine *rankness* of Eliot's style, its excess of physicality, that denies her the possibility of a seemingly unphysical masculine 'enduring vitality'. Feminine multiplicity and *différance* are seen once more as unwelcome supplements to single and whole masculine 'vitality'.

The sense implied by Bennett that George Eliot's male disguise of a 'rude' and 'aggressive' style represented a threat to the 'genuinely masculine' is a common thread running through much early Eliot criticism. While those who revered her person felt the need to praise her with the term 'feminine', those who were critical of her writing could use the same label as a means of diminishing her importance. To call Eliot's writing 'feminine', it seems, was a way of preserving authentic masculinity – and the professional activity of writing – for men. A review of John Cross's *Life* of Eliot, for example, took the biography as evidence of 'how impressionable, how emotional, how illogical, how feminine she was. . . . The person whom superficial critics long took to be the most masculine of her sex was a very woman' (*Heritage* 487). And Richard Simpson, in remarks that set down more explicitly than usual exactly why Eliot was a threat to conventional notions of masculinity, wrote in 1863 that Eliot, unlike other women, 'grasps at direct power through reasoning and speech. Having thus taken up the male position, the male ideal becomes hers, – the ideal of power' (*Heritage* 241).

The insistence that Eliot's writing was transparently and essentially feminine extended even to judgements of her literary characters. A common complaint was that Eliot, because she was a woman, did not have a sufficiently wide experience to portray men in her fiction (the implication being that the breadth of male experience did give men the ability to present female characters). One fear that seems to underlie this charge, as Edmond Scherer's remarks about Eliot's fiction illustrate, is that both masculine and feminine sexuality are somehow threatened when depicted by a woman:

> You must not look in her pages for the troubles, the excitements, the disorders of love. . . . A woman cannot sketch a man's passions, because she cannot feel them;

and as for painting those of her own sex, she would have to begin by unsexing herself to dare to take the public into confidence as to the last secrets of the feminine heart.[17]

According to Scherer, masculine sexuality is for the woman unknowable, while feminine sexuality, like the mysteries underlying the sybil's knowledge, exists only by remaining secret, by being repressed: if a woman writes of her sexuality, she will lose it – will become, indeed, like Lady Macbeth; 'unsexed'.

Many nineteenth-century readers responded to Eliot's portrayal of male characters in language of extreme and resentful mockery, as if these characters – like Eliot herself – were attacks on the very idea of masculinity. Robert Louis Stevenson, for example, asked of a friend who had written about George Eliot,

Did you – I forget – did you have a kick at the stern works of that melancholy puppy and humbug Daniel Deronda himself? – the Prince of Prigs; the literary abomination of desolation in the way of manhood; a type which is enough to make a man forswear the love of women, if that is how it must be gained. . . . Hats off all the same, you understand: a woman of genius.[18]

Here Stevenson uses the epithet 'woman of genius' both to intensify his attack on Eliot and to withdraw it by invoking the separate and laughable standards by which women were judged.

Close to Stevenson's point of view about Deronda was the more generalised theory that Eliot's heroes, like herself writing under a male pseudonym, were really women in disguise. In 1890, William Ernest Henley spoke of a sceptical male reader whose

sense of sex was strong enough to make him deny the possibility in any stage of being of nearly all the govern-

esses in revolt it pleased [Eliot] to put forward as men; for
with very few exceptions he knew they were heroes of the
divided skirt.

Henley's casting of Eliot's heroes as women led him to call
up particularly threatening or negative images of femininity: he described Deronda as 'an incarnation of woman's
rights', Tito Melema of *Romola* as 'an improper female in
breeches', and Silas Marner as 'a good, perplexed old maid'.
Henley clearly could not reconcile the liberality of Deronda,
the evil of Tito, or the vulnerability of Marner with his own
conception of masculinity – and so he transformed them
into images of the feminine lying outside the sphere of male
sexual domination: the feminist who seeks power inappropriate for women, the 'improper' woman who expresses her
sexuality without submitting to the restraints of marriage,
and the old maid, whose domain remains separate from
those dictated for women by partiarchy. Ironically, the only
male character whom Henley assumed to have 'the true
male principle about him' was Tertius Lydgate of *Middlemarch*, a figure whom Eliot presents as flawed for his sexism
and his resulting attraction to superficial and destructive
women (*Century* 161).

A similar insistence that the unlikeable qualities in Eliot's
male characters are really evidence of female transvestism
appears in Leslie Stephen's famous 1902 book on Eliot for
the English Men of Letters series. Stephen reported that
Eliot was 'too thoroughly feminine to be quite at home in
the psychology of the male animal'. He called Stephen
Guest of *The Mill on the Floss* 'a mere hairdresser's block'
and Tito Melema 'thoroughly and to his fingers' end a
woman'. Henley had not explained why he thought Tito
feminine, but Stephen offered a revealing explanation for
this attitude. Tito, he reported, 'is not cruel out of mere
badness, but from effeminacy'. This presumed 'effeminacy'
was linked in Stephen's mind to Tito's skill in achieving

power through deceptiveness rather than through physical force. He spoke of Tito as 'of the material of which the Delilahs are made, the treacherous, caressing, sensuous creatures who involve strong men in their meshes'. Stephen admired Tito only when he acted in a direct physical way:

> When he is fairly driven into a corner, . . . he can show his claws and act, for once, like a man. But his general position among his more violent associates is like that of a beautiful and treacherous woman who makes delicate caressing and ingenious equivocation do the work of the rougher and more downright masculine methods. [19]

Stephen's version of sexual difference assigns to woman not passivity but a dangerous and subversive weapon: in opposition to masculine physical force is a treacherous female sensuality that deceives and entraps. It is not surprising, therefore, that Stephen, like Henley, admired what he considered to be the manliness of Lydgate. Such a reading equates the characteristics of Rosamond Vincy with feminine sexuality and posits essential masculinity as its victim. Cecil's birchrod is for Stephen the female body imaged as a subtly netted trap: the phallic mother has become a seductress.

In the latter years of the twentieth century, much criticism of George Eliot – rather than mocking her – has de-sexed her by ignoring altogether the issue of gender. The underlying assumption that Eliot's femininity was a mark of weakness has continued in significant ways to operate, however. Though the iconography of the man-woman may now be muted, in other words, a sense that Eliot's intellectual activity was somehow in conflict with her gender still governs much thinking about her. In 1947, F.E. Baily detected in Eliot both 'female persistence' and female obstinacy and declared she had 'an enormous capacity for taking pains and acquiring facts, most unusual in a woman'. In her biography of 1960, Margaret Crompton repeated the com-

monplace that 'there was a combination in [Eliot's] make-up
of masculine intellect and feminine temperament', and Walter
Allen declared in 1964, 'However well-disciplined and "masculine" her mind might be, she was at the mercy of her
emotions, perhaps at the mercy of her need for affection and
self-sacrifice'. Even U.C. Knoepflmacher has contributed in a
small way to a gendered mode of thinking about George Eliot.
In his influential *Religious Humanism and the Victorian Novel*,
he attributed to her 'an almost masculine mastery of the
physical sciences'.[20]

Knoepflmacher's was only a passing remark, however. In
contrast, a major critic whose work consistently and aggressively has presented Eliot in rigidly gendered terms is Gordon
S. Haight, whose 1968 biography continues to be praised,
even by one feminist, for its scholarship and its objectivity.[21]
In his early book on George Eliot's relationship with John
Chapman (1940), Haight announced in his Preface that
Eliot's whole life, with all its 'strange contradictions', could
be explained by invoking the phrenological reading of
Eliot's skull cast by her friend Charles Bray, which declared
that Marian Evans always needed 'some one to lean upon'
and that she 'was not fitted to stand alone'.[22] Haight was not
the first to take Bray's interpretation as scientific fact, but
he is certainly the most influential scholar to have done so.
In all of his biographical writing about Eliot, Haight uses
Bray's comments as a leitmotif – a collection of phrases to
be invoked when seeking to explain or understand the
significant moments of Eliot's life, especially those that
involved her relationships with men: the death of Eliot's
father left her with no one to lean upon; the troubled relationship with the publisher John Chapman led Eliot to see
that he was not someone to lean upon; the friendship with
the philosopher Herbert Spencer, suspected by some at the
time to have been an engagement, led to the discovery that
Spencer too could not be leaned upon; the fulfilling relationship with the journalist and scientist George Henry

Lewes was the discovery, after years of searching, of someone to lean upon; the death of Eliot's editor John Blackwood left her professionally with no one to lean upon;
Eliot's marriage to John Cross proved that she was not fitted
to stand alone.[23] Haight also works Bray's imagery of feminine weakness into the chapter headings of his biography
and even into his imagined descriptions of physical action.
Take, for example, his account of the scandalous trip Eliot
made with Lewes to Europe in 1854, an act that effectively
cut her off from most social and family contacts: 'Like
Maggie and Stephen Guest aboard the Dutch vessel, Marian
paced up and down the deck, leaning on George's arm. . . .
At last she had found someone to lean upon' (GE 148).

Haight's perpetuation of Bray's essentialist assumptions
about Eliot's feminine dependency is not confined to his
habit of echoing the phrases of the phrenological reading. A
more subtle and pervasive form of the same endorsement
can be seen in Haight's tendency, especially when presenting Eliot's decisions having to do with men, to dramatise
her thoughts by using her own fictional device of free indirect discourse – something he never does when treating
other aspects of her life. Consider the description of Eliot's
decision to earn her living as a writer in London, made soon
after her father's funeral and during her first trip to Europe:

Alone, in the romantic town of her dream, Mary Ann
could now rest her frayed nerves and take stock of her
life. What was she to do? . . . [Her brother] Isaac had no
sympathy with Mary Ann's ideas or her feelings; if he
were to help, she would have to do things his way; he was
certainly not a man she could lean upon. But no other had
appeared ready to take the responsibility. She would be
thirty in November. She had never been good looking,
had none of the superficial charms that attract young
men. . . . No, she must find work to support herself. But
what? (GE 70–1)

In Haight's fictionalised presentation, Eliot decided to write only by default because she was too ugly to find a husband who would take 'responsibility' for her. A similar dramatising technique characterises Haight's account of Eliot's decision to return to the *Westminster Review* after her first difficult encounter with the philandering John Chapman:

> it was all too clear that John Chapman would never be the man she could lean upon. Still, to live in London, helping him unobtrusively with the *Review* would be better than never seeing him.
>   But how could it be contrived? (*GE* 90)

Again, Eliot's actions are seen as motivated not by professional concerns but by the need for someone to lean upon. The return to the *Review*, an association that gave Eliot contact with some of the most advanced thinkers of her day, is presented as merely a *contrivance* allowing her to be near Chapman.

An emphasis on dependence also characterises Haight's depiction of Eliot's famous relationship with George Henry Lewes. Repeatedly, when Haight describes Eliot and Lewes making a trip because Eliot felt the need to travel, we are told that 'Lewes [carried] her off', as if she were unable to move on her own (*GE* 338, 361, 374, 382). When Lewes himself was in a bad condition, however – as he often was – Haight reports that the two 'set out' together (*GE* 423). Lewes is never made by Haight the *object* of Eliot's ministrations in the way that she is made the object of his, in spite of the fact that it was Lewes who was in a state of nervous collapse when he and Eliot first went to Europe, that he was often in such states afterwards, and that Eliot on many occasions wrote or proofread for Lewes when his mental or physical health was bad. In this context, it is worth noting that the only time Eliot actually described herself as leaning on someone, she was referring not to Lewes, or even to a man, but rather to Mme d'Albert Durade, whose maternal attentions Eliot first enjoyed when she travelled to Europe after her father died. 'I call her always "maman",' Eliot wrote to her sister in 1850, 'and she is just the creature one loves to lean on and be petted by' (*GEL* 1: 328).

The effect of Haight's emphasis on the idea of Eliot's feminine dependence on men has been overwhelming. Bray's quasi-scientific diagnosis, endorsed by Haight, has been transformed into incontrovertible fact. In 1975 Neil Roberts spoke of 'the George Eliot we know from biographical sources, who was "always requiring some one to lean upon"'. Two years later, Joseph Wiesenfarth alluded confidently to 'the ardent woman whose biography shows that she was not fitted to stand alone'. As recently as 1980, Kathleen Adams entitled the last chapter of her book, 'Someone to Lean on, Someone to Love'. And surprisingly, even feminist critics Sandra Gilbert and Susan Gubar momentarily assumed Haight's tone and way of thinking when they called Eliot's marriage to John Cross 'the saddest sign of her inability to stand alone'. Finally, in the most blatant example of the tautological thinking that has created this image of George Eliot, John Purkis recently called Bray's phrenological reading an 'acute diagnosis' because it 'compares quite well with some of the psychological analyses of George Eliot which are to be found in modern biographies'.[24] What Haight and others assumed to be true on the authority of Charles Bray is now given new credence because Bray anticipated what Haight and others would say. Each diagnosis validates the other.

Because Bray's interpretation of Eliot's character has had more influence on her biographies than any other single opinion, it seems worth quoting at some length. Bray based his diagnosis, published five years after Eliot's death, on a cast allegedly taken of her skull in 1844, which, he remarked proudly, 'is still in my possession':

Miss Evans's head is a very large one, 22 ¼ inches round;
George Combe, on first seeing the cast, took it for a
man's. The temperament, nervous lymphatic, that is,
active without endurance, and her working hours were
never more than from 9 a.m. till 1 p.m. The third
volume of Strauss was very heavy work to her, and she
required much encouragement to keep her up to it. In her
brain-development the Intellect greatly predominates; it
is very large, more in length than in its peripheral surface.
In the Feelings, the Animal and Moral regions are about
equal; the moral being quite sufficient to keep the animal
in order and in due subservience, but would not be spontaneously active. The social feelings were very active,
particularly the adhesiveness. She was of a most affectionate disposition, always requiring some one to lean upon,
preferring what has hitherto been considered the stronger
sex, to the other and more impressible. She was not fitted
to stand alone. Her sense of character – of men and
things, is a predominantly intellectual one.[25]

Bray's allusions to the size of Eliot's skull, to the 'nervous
lymphatic' temperament that is 'active without endurance',
to the 'heavy' burden that translation became for Eliot, and
to the contrast between 'the stronger sex' and the 'more impressible' one – all these echo the language of nineteenth-
century gender theories, which also often assumed the tones
and terminology of scientific discourse in order to assert
their *a priori* notions about feminine weakness. The emphasis on Eliot's body is familiar as well: this time quite
literally, her mind is reduced to a physical specimen whose
mould has been laid out for scientific analysis.

Bray's language is not, however, uniformly scientific,
even in a loose sense of that word. A striking feature of his
description is its shifting verb tenses and its analogous
sliding between impersonal and personal nouns or pronouns: the 'scientific' diagnosis, allegedly based on the still

present evidence of the skull cast, is written in the present tense and using impersonal nouns or pronouns ('it', 'the Temperament', 'the Intellect', etc.), but is continually undercut by Bray's subjective memories, described in the past tense and indicated by the use of personal pronouns ('she' or 'her'). Bray's attention seems, in fact, to hover between the cast in front of him and the mental picture he has conjured up of the woman he had known decades earlier – and the two visions seem continually to modify each other. The verbal and logical ambiguities of Bray's style thus anticipate the circular logic of Haight's own use of Bray's observations: just as Haight and Bray validate each other, so Bray's memories give credibility to his empirical observations – and vice versa. Even if phrenology had scientific validity, Bray's method would be seriously open to question.

It should be pointed out, moreover, that Haight's choice of Charles Bray as his authority on Eliot's character is problematic from more than a scientific point of view: in addition to the fact that Bray saw little of her after she became a novelist, it should be remembered that, by his own admission, the two often had 'violent quarrels' and that she taunted him more than once both for his commitment to phrenology and for his retrograde ideas about women.[26] It is not surprising, therefore, that Bray should have used the language of phrenology as a device to express his own patriarchal judgements about George Eliot. That Haight and other Eliot scholars should have embraced this view of her, above all others, seems also a telling reflection of their own preoccupations and fears: the female novelist and sage must ultimately be reduced to feminine weakness – the common feature of Eliot iconography in all its variations.

When writing a biography, it might be asked, how is one to escape being influenced by personal preoccupations? The answer, of course, is that such avoidance is impossible.

What most weakens Haight's and other biographies of Eliot, therefore, is not that they are biased, but that they exhibit no awareness of their own biases and limitations: these writers present interpretations as if they were objective and indisputable facts, and many of their readers have accepted this equation. The result is that Eliot's character and life have often been interpreted according to essentialist assumptions about feminine weakness and dependence. What would the result be, however, if an account of Eliot's biography began with the premise that gender differences are merely constructions of patriarchal culture? By rejecting essentialist gender definitions exactly where earlier critics have accepted or assumed them, would the biographer make from the same materials a very different interpretation? It is my intention in Chapter 2 briefly to explore this possibility. I have not attempted to add any new *information* to the already crowded field of Eliot biography; nor do I make any claims to objectivity. Assuming, on the contrary, that *all* biography is interpretation, I intend to look at the primary materials of Eliot's life as a collection of texts that invite different readings depending on the ideological premises of the reader.

My premises are those of a feminist critic who rejects essentialist gender definitions. My intention is not to ignore gender difference, but rather to see it as culturally constructed and to consider Eliot's life, therefore, in terms of her overdetermined position as a feminine gendered subject within patriarchy. In such a culture, female desire is invisible and unacknowledged, for the woman is constructed as the mediator of desire between men – a notion interestingly supported by Scherer's assumption that when a woman describes feminine sexuality she unsexes herself. As Luce Irigaray has argued, patriarchal culture depends on an 'hom(m)o-sexual monopoly' in which 'the use and traffic in women' supports a masculine power structure that maintains its supremacy by 'speculations . . . and more or

less rivalrous appropriations' between men. Hom(m)o-
sexuality, according to Irigaray, 'is played out through the
bodies of women', and heterosexuality is 'just an alibi for
the smooth workings of man's relation with himself, of
relations among men'. In such a culture, homosexuality is
taboo, and heterosexual relations merely reinforce the
bonds of power between men; woman has three possible
functions – virgin, mother, or whore – and in all of these
roles she is the object of masculine desire, not a desiring
subject.[27]

The repression of the female subject and the relegation of
her to the status of commodity in an economic exchange
between men make the position of the woman writer an
especially problematic one. If woman is programmed by
culture to deny her own subjectivity, then what is her
relation to language and to writing? When the woman tries
to publish her work and so to enter the male *profession* of
writing, moreover, the difficulty is still more intense.
Especially in the nineteenth century, as N. N. Feltes has
pointed out, '"woman writer" and "professional" were
constructed as contradictory concepts'.[28] For this reason,
the life of Marian Evans, the woman who defied the
conventions of marriage and published under the male
pseudonym 'George Eliot', can be seen as a site of enormous
tension – one stage on which the contradictions of patriarchal culture were enacted.

2 Woman Writing: George Eliot's Life

Born in 1819, Mary Ann Evans – who was later to assume the names 'Marian Evans', 'Marian Lewes' and 'George Eliot' – was the third child and second daughter of Christiana Pearson Evans and Robert Evans of Warwickshire. Biographies of George Eliot have, with a few exceptions, ignored the influence of Pearson Evans on her daughter, while elaborating at length on the father's impact. In part, this imbalance can be attributed to the fact that Pearson Evans died when Eliot was only sixteen years old: there is simply not much evidence about their relationship. This fact does not account, however, for the extent to which Eliot's mother has been demonised by those biographers who do not ignore her. A common theory is that the birth of Pearson Evans's third child harmed her health, that she blamed the young Mary Ann for this, and that she punished her by sending her to boarding school at the age of five. The theory of maternal rejection can be traced back to an earlier assumption – based on comments by Eliot's husband, John Cross – that Pearson Evans is the original for some of Eliot's unpleasant and tyrannical characters: Mrs Hackit of *Scenes of Clerical Life*, Mrs Poyser of *Adam Bede*, and the Dodson sisters of *The Mill on the Floss*. There is no evidence, however, that these characters were perfectly accurate portraits of Pearson Evans rather than simply representative depictions of her social class. In any case, we cannot be sure of the truth of any of the hypotheses about Eliot's mother.

Something that biographers have failed to analyse at any length, moreover, is that whether or not Eliot's mother rejected her, Pearson Evans died before her daughter had reached adulthood: *loss* of the mother was a fact in Eliot's life even if maternal rejection was not. From this perspective, it is interesting that Eliot referred in several letters to the trauma she suffered at her mother's death and that in her school notebook, kept during roughly the time when her mother was ill, she copied down from several sources poems about the deaths of young people, including one about the death of a young wife.[1] Eliot's interest in these poems has been ridiculed as evidence of her adolescent sentimentality, but it might also be an expression of her suppressed grief at the grave illness of her young mother. If there is any truth in the idea that Eliot was always desperately seeking affection, this may well have been a response to the early loss, whenever and however it occurred, of her mother's love. It is worth noting, too, that Eliot's fiction contains, as Karen Mann has pointed out, an unusual number of deathbed scenes involving mothers or feminine men and that pathos in her fiction is often linked with loss of the pre-Oedipal union with the mother.[2] Maternal love appears in both Eliot's life and her fiction as a significant and tantalising gap.

What can be known about Pearson Evans, however, is that her death had many practical consequences for the young Mary Ann. Before her mother's illness, she had boarded at three different schools over a period of ten years and had formed several intense friendships, especially one with Maria Lewis, principal governess of Mrs Wallington's school in Nuneaton. In these female communities, Eliot had excelled in her work and had won the regard and affection of many of her fellow students. In 1835, however, when both her parents were taken ill, Eliot left her school and returned to her family. Several months later, Pearson Evans died, and in the following year Eliot's older sister Chrissey was married. These events altered altogether Eliot's position in life: while the sons in the Evans family inherited property and professional responsibility, the daughters inherited domestic feminine tasks, but had no rights to the family homes. Eliot's older half-sister Fanny, for example, moved at the age of fourteen to become her older brother Robert's housekeeper when he took over his father's former job at Kirk Hallam, Derbyshire. She did not live in her own house until she married and after her husband's death had to board with her widowed sister-in-law. The younger sister Chrissey also had difficulties acquiring a home. When her husband had financial difficulties, her father bought the small house she occupied with her family, but when Evans died, her brother Isaac, not Chrissey, inherited the house. Though Isaac eventually allowed Chrissey to live in the house rent-free, he kept control of it and her finances. Installing himself as the new patriarch, he even refused to let Chrissey take care of her own bills (*GEL* 8: 221). Eliot's case was somewhat different from those of her sisters, but it too involved submitting to masculine authority. The patriarchal laws of primogeniture left her, the single daughter, without property and in the position of playing sole housekeeper, companion and nurse to her father until his death, which took place in 1849, when she was twenty-nine years old.

During the intervening years, Eliot suffered acutely. As Cross noted with surprising frankness about her first years as housekeeper,

> it requires no great effort of imagination to conceive that this life . . . was, as a matter of fact, very monotonous, very difficult, very discouraging. It could scarcely be otherwise to a young girl, with a full passionate nature and hungry intellect, shut up in a farmhouse in the remote country.[3]

While Eliot pursued this domestic life, Robert Evans's ambitions for the future were invested in his younger son Isaac, who, when he was married in 1841, inherited his father's job as agent of the Arbury estates as well as the accompanying right to occupy Griff House, the family dwelling, where Eliot had been housekeeper since Chrissey's marriage. Eliot's letters during Isaac's courtship reveal a full awareness of her difficult predicament as it became increasingly clear that her prospective sister-in-law would usurp her place at Griff: in the musical chairs of patriarchal family relationships, the single daughter loses her place when new women marry into the family. Eliot wrote bitterly to Maria Lewis, 'there seems a probability of my being an unoccupied damsel, of my being severed from all the ties that have hitherto given my existence the semblance of a usefulness beyond that of making up the requisite quantum of animal matter in the universe' (*GEL* 1: 50). In Cross's words, Isaac's marriage created 'a change almost amounting to a revolution in Miss Evans's life'.[4]

After Isaac's marriage, the Evans family devoted itself more and more to promoting Eliot's status as commodity in the marriage market. Robert Evans had wanted to spend his retirement in a small cottage in the country, but felt the necessity of making Eliot available for eligible husbands by renting a respectable house in Coventry. The move to the city did not fulfil these expectations, however. First, Eliot befriended there a lively group of intellectuals who used to gather at the home of Charles and Cara Bray. She had been brought to the Bray home by Charles's sister, Elizabeth Pears, who was hoping that Eliot, who had gone through an intense evangelical phase in her adolescence, would influence Charles and his brother-in-law Charles Hennell to reconsider their radical stance that there was no supernatural basis for Christianity. The influence (if any was necessary) went in the other direction, however, and Eliot herself became convinced that Christianity, like other religions, was a product of culture. Scripture, she concluded, was not divinely revealed but rather was a collection of 'histories consisting of mingled truth and fiction', while Christian doctrine was 'most pernicious in its influence on individual and social happiness' (*GEL* 1: 128). In 1842, therefore, less than a year after the move to Coventry, Eliot announced to her father that she would not go to church with him.

What followed was a family drama that reveals the close relationship of patriarchal religion to the power relations in the marriage market-place. Robert Evans was appalled by Eliot's adamant refusal, but for social reasons rather than for religious ones. He believed – by Cara Bray's account, at Isaac's instigation (*GEL* 1: 156–7) – that Eliot's religious heterodoxy, as well as her association with such radical thinkers as the Brays and the Hennells, would jeopardise her marital prospects. Isaac therefore undertook to '[*school*] Mary Ann' (*GEL* 1: 129, n. 4) by informing her that she was squandering the family investment in her future: without a religious affiliation, her already diminishing commodity value as marriageable virgin was seriously threatened.

Eliot's response was indignant and confident. Declaring she 'could not be happy to remain as an incubus or an unjust absorber of your hardly earned gains which might be better applied among my Brothers and Sisters with their children', she volunteered, in the event that her father disinherited her or refused to live with her, to 'rely on my own energies and resources feeble as they are' (*GEL* 1: 129). Her plan, according to Cross, was to 'go into lodgings at Leamington and to try to support herself by teaching' (*GEL* 1: 131, n. 8). That Eliot knew the consequences of such a decision is clear from her earlier correspondence with Maria Lewis, in which a frequent topic was Lewis's precarious social and financial position as a single governess seeking employment. But such a move would also have been the only possible escape at the time from Eliot's powerless position in her family, where her value was determined entirely by her marriageability, or, failing that, by her temporary usefulness as a caretaker for her father. Her marriage seemed all the more necessary to her family, moreover, after Robert

Evans took £800 from his daughters' inheritance to help Christiana's husband out of his financial troubles.

During the difficult weeks that followed Eliot's refusal to go to church, she was sent to stay with Isaac, and Evans made arrangements to give up his tenancy of the house in Coventry. Eventually, however, the father and daughter struck a compromise: Eliot would attend services with her father if he would ask no questions about her beliefs. After this, Eliot led a kind of double life, tending her father much of the time, but also enjoying the intellectual atmosphere provided by the Brays and their many friends. The years in Coventry also marked the beginning of Eliot's publishing career. In 1843, she was an attendant at the marriage of Rufa Brabant to Charles Hennell, Cara Bray's brother. Rufa had undertaken to translate for publication David Friedrich Strauss's *Life of Jesus*, a work that challenged the divinity of Christ. When Rufa found the task too much to handle, Eliot took it over and spent the next two years working almost daily to produce a publication on whose title page her name never appeared and for which she was paid a meagre £20. Even at this early stage of her literary career, moreover, Eliot was confronted by a defensive self-loathing at taking up the masculine professional position: she expressed regret that Strauss had learned the translation was being done by a '*young lady*' and wrote to Cara Bray, 'I am sure he must have some twinges of alarm to think he was dependent on that most contemptible specimen of the human being for his English reputation' (*GEL* 1: 177). In spite of this, however, Eliot's achievement was not small. As Hilary Fraser has pointed out, 'the translation . . . had a devastating effect on Victorian faith'.[5] Eliot may still have been attending church on Sundays with her father, but she spent her weekdays radically undermining the tenets of Christianity.

All of her time was not spent at translation, however. Eliot continued to enjoy a social life at Rosehill, the home of the Brays, where in 1848 she made a strong impression on Ralph Waldo Emerson. She also did some travelling, including a trip of a few weeks to the home of Rufa Brabant's parents. The visit, which took place soon after Rufa's marriage, turned out to be a difficult and embarrassing one. Eliot enjoyed the intellectual comradeship of Dr Brabant – something she could not share with her father – and reported delightedly to Cara Bray that he had named her 'Deutera', which she explained as a 'learned pun . . . which *means* second and *sounds* a little like daughter' (*GEL* 1: 164). The evidence suggests, however, that Brabant's fatherly attentions soon turned sexual, and Eliot was eventually asked by Mrs Brabant to leave.

There is a long tradition in Eliot biography of citing the Brabant incident as an early instance of a lifelong pattern whereby, in Haight's words, 'an intellectual friendship drawn by over-ready expansiveness into feelings misunderstood' recalls 'that phrenological cast with its moral regions sufficient to keep the animal in due subservience, but not spontaneously active' (*GE* 52). Haight bases his diagnosis on an account in the diary of the *Westminster Review*'s editor John Chapman, which in turn was based on the oral reports of Rufa Brabant Hennell. While calling Brabant 'the chief cause of all that passed', Chapman saw at the heart of the situation Eliot's 'simplicity of . . . heart and her ignorance of (or incapability of practising) the required conventionalisms' (quoted in *GE* 50).

Both these readings need to be contextualised, however. As usual, Haight is returning to Charles Bray's analysis of Eliot's character, while Chapman's account – given the fact that he attempted an extra-marital liaison with Eliot a few years after the Brabant incident and so was hardly himself an observer of 'the required conventionalisms' – is not entirely to be trusted. It is impossible to know, of course, exactly what happened between Brabant and Eliot, nor does it matter. It seems worthwhile, however, to try to interpret Eliot's position with regard to Brabant in terms of assumptions that do not depend – as both Haight's and Chapman's do – on artificial oppositions between the animal and the moral or between the naive and the conventional, labels applied more to female sexual behaviour than to male. For example, one possible reason why Eliot in a number of instances found herself in a compromising situation with men was precisely the fact that she occupied an impossible double position as an intellectual woman with sexual desires. The standard interpretation of Eliot's problematic relationship with Brabant offers one more example of the way in which patriarchy places the burden of its own moral code on the woman – and on the repression of her sexuality.

Whatever happened between Eliot and Brabant, moreover – and it may have been very little – she did eventually regard the relationship with some irony. Less frequently quoted than Chapman's and Haight's appraisals are her own comments, made to Sara Hennell:

> I am too inflatedly conceited to think it worth my while to run after Dr. Brabant or his correspondence. If I ever offered incense to him it was because there was no other deity at hand and because I wanted some kind of worship pour passer le temps. I always knew that I could belabour my fetisch if I chose, and laughed at him in my sleeve. Even that degree of inclination towards mock reverence has long since passed away and ridiculous as it may seem to every one else, I looked on my renewal of a correspondence with him as a favour *conferred* by me rather than *received*. (*GEL* 1: 225)

Here Eliot uses the imagery of religious worship to mock her own responses to Brabant and then turns the tables on him, making herself the object of reverence and him the humble worshipper. It is worth noting, too, that in 1847 Eliot turned down Brabant's invitation to travel to Germany with him. Haight, incidentally, fails to take this fact as evidence that Eliot did *not* always need someone to lean upon.

Nor does Haight give such a reading to the fact that Eliot was briefly courted in 1845 by a young picture restorer. Though the information about this relationship is sparse, it is clear from extant letters that Eliot at first encouraged the young man, only to realise that, in Cara Bray's words, 'she could never love or respect him enough to marry him and that it would involve too great a sacrifice of her mind and pursuits. So she wrote to him to break it off' (*GEL* 1: 184). At the age of twenty-five – by Victorian standards rather old for the marriage market – Eliot put her 'mind and pursuits' before the need to have a man to support her or someone to lean upon. And this was the case in spite of the fact that during these important years of her young woman-hood, in addition to tending to her housekeeping duties, Eliot spent much of her time taking care of her father, often with emotionally taxing results. On one occasion, for example, she was called back by her brother from a vacation in Scotland when her father broke his leg. More than three years before his death, Cara Bray wrote to her sister Sara Hennell that Robert Evans's illness had seriously 'tried' Eliot because 'for all the time she had for rest and fresh air, she had to read to him' (*GEL* 1: 206). In the last year of his life, Cara was even franker about Eliot's position in relation to her father:

poor M.A., alone with him, has the whole care and fatigue of nursing him night and day. . . . It is a great comfort that he is now quite aware of his situation, and was not in the least discomposed when Isaac told him he might die suddenly . . . ; and he takes opportunities now of saying kind things to M.A., contrary to his wont. Poor girl, it shows how rare they are by the gratitude with which she re-peats the commonest expressions of kindness. (*GEL* 1: 272)

Eliot herself did not analyse the situation with Cara's distance and candour, but her letters still reveal that there was
a tension between her sense of duty toward her father and
her need to pursue her own interests. Often, she seems to
have placed her father's demands before 'my own pleasure'
and 'my own bent' (*GEL* 1: 256, 263), but with difficulty.
In 1841, she wrote to Maria Lewis, 'My dear Father has just
returned rather sooner than I expected and has limited my
allowance of time for writing' (*GEL* 1: 121). Five years
later, when she expressed a similar sentiment to Sara Hennell, her language had become charged with guilt, resent-
ment and sarcasm: 'I am sinning against my daddy, by
yielding to the strong impulse I felt to write to you, for he
looks at me as if he wanted me to read to him, so farewell,
meine liebe' (*GEL* 1: 223–4). Here both the act of writing
and the intimacy with Sara, expressed by the lover's phrase
'meine liebe', stand in sinful conflict with the 'daddy's'
patriarchal demands. To do the moral thing, in these terms,
is to regress into the infantile – and to retreat both from
female friendship and from writing.

It is not surprising, therefore, that when Eliot's father
actually was close to death in 1849, she felt acute panic at
the loss of this controlling presence. She wrote to the Brays,
'What shall I be without my Father? It will seem as if a part
of my moral nature were gone. I had a horrid vision of
myself last night becoming earthly sensual and devilish for
want of that purifying restraining influence' (*GEL* 1: 284).
Precisely what Eliot feared in herself at her father's death is
impossible to define, but it is tempting to speculate. Nina
Auerbach sees this moment as 'a baptism into transcendent
new incarnations': 'The spinsterhood inaugurated by loss of
family repeats in little her renunciation of God, throwing
her into a chaos of identity, demonic not merely in its
potential sensuality but in its infinite potentiality of selves'.[6]
In my view, however, it seems unwarranted to bestow upon
Eliot a romantic kind of spinsterdom after her father's

death, when she had in fact been suffering the negative consequences of her single state for many years: if Eliot had married, like all four of her siblings, she would not have spent most of her twenties singly tending her father.

Auerbach's emphasis on the positive aspects of the 'demonic' break from paternal authority is intriguing, however. When Robert Evans was alive, his authority seemed generally to override the private 'pleasure' of 'strong impulse', but Eliot anticipates without him not only a devilish self but also an unpurified, unrestrained, 'sensual' and 'earthly' one as well – a perception at some level, perhaps, that woman's escape from patriarchal ties implies a return to the female body, to a satisfaction of desire without recourse to masculine definitions. Such a state might be compared to that of the narcissistic woman, who, in Jacobus's words, stands as a 'threat' to patriarchy because 'she may reveal the primacy of narcissism, undercutting object love and mimetic desire alike'.[7] To Eliot, whose life for three decades had been governed so pervasively by her father, this sudden freedom from masculine definitions may well have been a terrifying prospect.

Robert Evans's will granted his position and properties in Derbyshire to his elder son Robert and those in Warwickshire to Isaac. His two elder daughters, each of whom had already received £1,000 when she married, received another £1,000, as well as some household goods. Eliot – because she was still unmarried and so was assumed unable to manage her own inheritance – received £2,000 to be held in trust for her by her brothers and the family lawyer. She also was assigned £100 in cash to compensate her for the household goods that her sisters received. With this money, Eliot was able to set off less than two weeks after her father's death on a trip to the Continent with the Brays – free for the first time in her life to travel where and when she chose. Six weeks later, the Brays returned to England, leaving Eliot on her own in Geneva, where she spent most of the next eight months.

Eliot's letters from Geneva reveal that this was an immensely difficult time for her, but they indicate as well that she quickly formed strong and lasting ties with the D'Albert Durades, the family in whose *pension* she lived much of the time. Toward Madame D'Albert, as I have already indicated, Eliot felt an intense daughterly affection, while of M. D'Albert she reported, 'I love him already as if he were father and brother both'. In a short period of time, Eliot had thus been able to reconstitute – and to improve upon – her lost family: the mother she had lost as a girl, the father she had lost as a young woman, and the loving and understanding brother she had never found in the imperious Isaac. In a different way, she was also recreating the intellectual atmosphere that had sustained her at Rosehill: life with the D'Alberts included music, theatre, the reading aloud of poetry, and much companionship with their knowledgeable friends. After only two weeks with the D'Alberts, Eliot wrote to Cara Bray, 'I like these dear people better and better – everything is so in harmony with one's moral feeling that I really can almost say I never enjoyed a more complete bien-etre in my life than during the last fortnight' (*GEL* 1: 316).

When Eliot returned to England, however, she was coming back not to 'harmony' but to an excluding world in which she no longer had an established place: with the death of her father, she had lost her status as daughter, and she had failed to secure any husband as her new sponsor within patriarchy. In this uncertain state, after a visit with the Brays, she travelled to see her siblings, but with no intention of ever depending on them. She reported to Cara, in fact, that although she was fond of her sister Chrissey, 'I am delighted to feel that I am of no importance to any of them, and have no motive for living amongst them' (*GEL* 1: 336). Instead, Eliot was determining already that she would move to London and contemplated spending part of each year in Europe. By January of 1851, she had begun to carry out this plan by becoming a lodger in the London home of John Chapman, the publisher of Eliot's translation of Strauss and future editor of the *Westminster Review*, whom she had met at Rosehill. This move had professional implications for Eliot as well. She had already written one review for the *Westminster*, and after Chapman purchased the journal in May of 1851, she became, in effect, its shadow editor: though her name did not appear in the *Review* and she received almost no pay for her work there, Eliot wrote most of its prospectus and many of its articles, as well as making the important editorial decisions for Chapman, who had neither her discipline nor her organisational skills and who was perfectly content to exploit both her knowledge and her labour.

Nor did Chapman stop at making use of Eliot's mind. As has been well known since Haight's 1940 publication of Chapman's diaries, Chapman was an experienced philanderer and quickly invited Eliot to enjoy, along with his wife and mistress (his children's live-in governess), his sexual attentions. As with the case involving Dr Brabant, the facts of the Chapman liaison are difficult to ascertain. The information that is available comes almost exclusively from Chapman's diaries, which present the situation entirely from his point of view and could be partly fantasy or embellishment. Interpreting these diaries is made still more difficult by the fact that Haight and others have created a romantic image of Chapman as a 'magnetic' (the most repeated word about Chapman in biographical accounts) Svengali whose charms were irresistible to women. Though Haight calls Chapman at one point a 'fatuous man' and at another a 'contemptible wretch', his tone is generally more than half-admiring of Chapman's seductive skills, and he carefully stacks his cards by exaggerating both Chapman's positive attributes and Eliot's ugliness and awkwardness. In judging Eliot's behaviour with Chapman, Haight pulls out his old list of explanatory formulas about 'her unfortunately balanced moral and animal regions' (*GE* 86) and falls back on his technique of dramatising Eliot's thoughts in free indirect discourse. Typically, Haight's fantasies overwhelm his factual account and shift the emphasis away both from Eliot's professional interest in the *Westminster Review* and from Chapman's obvious pathology.

Yet Chapman's own patterns of behaviour deserve some serious scrutiny if one is to speculate about Eliot's responses to him. The diaries reveal that, however 'magnetic' Chapman may have been superficially, he was obsessed with manipulating and hurting women. Continually during 1851, the first year when Eliot was living in his house, Chapman provoked fights among his wife, his mistress, and Eliot and then assumed the role of placator. Many of his diary accounts create a picture of all three women trapped in a web sadistically woven by him. This entry is typical of Chapman's tendency to play the women off against each other while seeing himself as a victim of their caprices:

> Last night accompanied S. [his wife] and the Hardmetts to the Hullah concert, E. [his mistress] was kind to me before I went and kissed me several times. At parting she kissed me saying 'God bless thee thou frail bark!' But alas this morning she is all bitterness and icy coldness, the result I believe of conversation she had last night with M. [Eliot] – who was very severe and unjust to me yesterday.[8]

Chapman's sense of victimisation is expressed at another point in terms that echo and elaborate upon Bray's reading of Eliot's skull:

> It is the order of nature that women should lean on men, but men have none to lean upon, and hence the necessity preeminently in them of SELF-culture and by a closer relation to nature so nourish and strengthen themselves

by striking deep and extended roots in the spirit-world
that they may stand strong alone. Few women understand or sympathize with this need, but rather oppose its
fulfilment, and thus the spiritual nature of most men
withers now.[9]

It is worth noting here that Chapman's intellectual interests
did not prove to tend toward the 'spirit-world' that he
romantically associated with the superiority of men. After
giving up the *Westminster Review*, he received his MD in
1857 and six years later published a book entitled *Functional
Diseases of Women*. He devoted his medical practice entirely
to female ailments, including hysteria, all of which he
treated with the application of ice on the spine – a remedy
for which he claimed great success. He wrote to one ex-
mistress, 'I began to treat a girl who had on average *6 fits an
hour* (!) every day; from that, she has ceased to have fits,
except when she has neglected my orders'.[10] In his medical
practice as in his private life, it appears, John Chapman
needed to impose his will on women, while protecting what
he perceived to be his masculine 'spiritual nature'.

That George Eliot began to board in this man's home just
at the point when she had returned alone from Europe and
was beginning actively to pursue her interest in writing –
and that he should have been the means by which she could
publish her work and meet other people with the same
intellectual interests – must have led to difficulties for her. If
his diaries are accurate, Eliot did for a time suffer consider-
ably as a result of Chapman's fickle attentions. But the
outcome of the situation – contrary to Ruby Redinger's
unsupported theory that 'the physical attraction Chapman
had for her was stronger than she was to feel for any other
man' and that he 'had a meaning in her life which not even
her near-perfect companionship with Lewes could wholly
supplant'[11] – appears to have been that Eliot eventually
took control of herself and of her life. Withdrawing from

Chapman's destructive sexual games, she continued her professional association with him, writing for and effectively editing the *Review*. Eliot's correspondence with Chapman over the years, in which she addresses him in tones of increasing confidence and professionalism – as well as with occasional sarcasm – reveals, moreover, her growing ironic distance from him. When her close friend Barbara Bodichon became involved with Chapman in 1854, Eliot's response was not one of jealousy, but of sympathy for Bodichon's difficult position. As Rosalind Wade has suggested, Eliot's behaviour toward both Brabant and Chapman can be seen as a sign, not of weakness, but of extraordinary resilience.[12]

During the years that Eliot spent boarding in Chapman's house and working on the *Review*, she befriended the philosopher Herbert Spencer, with whom she often attended plays and concerts. The evidence suggests that Eliot was interested in a sexual relationship with Spencer – another indication, in Haight's view, of Eliot's inappropriately 'expansive affection' (*GE* 115) – but Spencer, who never married and developed increasingly paranoid theories about the inferiority of women, seemed afraid of physical passion. It was then some while after the failed affair with Spencer that Eliot began to spend time with George Henry Lewes, a married journalist whom she had met in October of 1851 (Lewes's wife had been conducting an extra-marital sexual relationship for some time and had just given birth to her lover's child – she was to bear four children by this man). Two years later, Eliot moved out of Chapman's house, presumably in order to have more privacy in her relationship with Lewes, and in July of 1854 she astonished most of her friends by leaving with him for Germany, where they spent approximately eight months. After they returned to England, the two openly lived together, calling themselves wife and husband, until Lewes died in 1878.

The story of the relationship of George Eliot and George

Henry Lewes is one of the most famous in nineteenth-century biography and from the beginning has invited a host of interpretations, many of which express the stereotypical double standard produced by woman's mediating position in patriarchy: an assertion of female heterosexual desire is judged immoral, while analogous behaviour in the male is admired as conquest. Not surprisingly, therefore, when Eliot and Lewes returned to England, Lewes was generally accepted socially, while Eliot was often excluded from respectable gatherings. Charles Eliot Norton described the situation as he saw it in 1869, fifteen years after Eliot and Lewes had begun living together:

> She is not received in general society, and the women who visit her are either so emancipée as not to mind what the world says about them, or have no social position to maintain. Lewes dines out a good deal, and some of the men with whom he dines go without their wives to his house on Sundays. No one whom I have heard speak, speaks in other than terms of respect of Mrs. Lewes, but the common feeling is that it will not do for society to condone so flagrant a breach as hers of a convention and a sentiment (to use no stronger terms) on which morality greatly relies for support. I suspect society is right in this. [13]

The argument for the contradiction that Norton so eloquently described and then condoned – in addition to its silent assumption that only women could be seen as guilty of sexual misbehaviour – depended on the related idea that respectable daughters and wives, as the sole bearers and upholders of sexual morality, had to be protected from Eliot's scandalous and polluting influence. Using the same logic, the phrenologist George Combe, who questioned Eliot's sanity after he had heard about the Lewes relationship (not a response he had to Charles Bray's philandering), worried about Eliot's effect on the sanctity of female virtue. He wrote to Bray,

> If you receive her into your family circle, . . . pray consider whether you will do justice to your own female domestic circle, and how other ladies may feel about going into a circle which makes no distinction between those who act thus, and those who preserve their honour unspotted? (*GEL* 8: 130)

Clearly Eliot's decision to express her sexuality without submitting to the forms of marriage was a challenge to the very structure of patriarchal culture, whose chief medium of exchange was 'unspotted' female 'honour'. In ceasing to act as currency between men, Eliot assumed the role of the masculine subject and so denied herself the right to a 'feminine' position in society.

The effects of this forfeiture were far-reaching. In addition to bringing upon herself the disapproval of many influential people – including even John Stuart Mill, the author of *On the Subjection of Women* – Eliot also suffered the embarrassment of being told that she and Lewes would not be welcome in a neighbourhood in Kent where they contemplated moving. When they purchased a house in Regent's Park, Eliot was profoundly hurt that their house-warming – for which she had ordered a lavish supper and hired musicians – was attended by a pathetically small number of people. Many of Eliot's friends assumed hypocritical or contradictory attitudes toward her. When Tennyson's memoirs were published in 1897, a brief mention of Mrs Tennyson's visit to the novelist was deleted (*GE* 439). Even Eliot's visit to Girton College – the first woman's college in the exclusive Oxbridge system, for whose founding Eliot had given a donation – was poisoned by moralistic self-righteousness: a reception planned in her honour was cancelled when the mistress learned of it.

Not surprisingly, Eliot's own brother was among those who condemned her actions. Even before he heard of Eliot's new situation, he had made her life difficult because she did not play the role of docile sister. When she visited Chrissey after her husband's death, for example, Isaac went into a 'violent passion' when Eliot left her sister before consulting him (*GEL* 2: 75). He also tried to dominate Eliot's attempts to withdraw her allotted money from her inheritance. In 1854, Eliot wrote to Bray about Isaac's 'disinclination to accommodate me' in her attempts to get her money from the trust that had been left her (*GEL* 2: 184). When Eliot finally informed Isaac of her relationship with Lewes, he responded with a letter from his lawyer which alleged that Isaac could not write to Eliot 'in a Brotherly Spirit' because he had not been fully informed of her 'altered state' (*GEL* 2: 346). In Isaac's view, even the brother–sister relationship was dependent on the woman's remaining physically intact and retaining her mediating place within patriarchy. For Eliot to live with a married man was, in this sense, to defy Isaac's own masculine power. Eliot's response to the letter from Isaac's lawyer, though she expressed privately that she had been greatly hurt by it, was as confident as her reply to her father after she had stopped going to church. Cleverly, she put the lawyer in his place by reminding him first of his position as a Trustee of *her* inheritance (*GEL* 2: 349–50). The price that Eliot had to pay for her offences against her brother was, none the less, severe. In addition to losing all contact with him, she was also cut off from the rest of her family – including Chrissey, who before she died of tuberculosis in 1859 expressed regret that she had submitted to her brother's will by not communicating with her wayward sister (*GE* 277).

Eliot's own response to her socially enforced exile was strong and cogent. Claiming a legitimacy for her relationship with Lewes, she adopted the name 'Mrs Lewes' (partly to protect herself from eviction by self-righteous landlords) and in every way played the role of a spouse – a role that in this case included supporting Lewes's wife, Agnes Jervis Lewes, and all of Jervis Lewes's children: the three sons she had by Lewes as well as the four children she had by her lover. Eliot saw with a clear and cynical eye the hypocrisy underlying her social ostracism. 'Light and easily broken ties,' she wrote to one friend, 'are what I neither desire theoretically nor could live for practically. Women who are satisfied with such ties do *not* act as I have done – they obtain what they desire and are still invited to dinner' (*GEL* 2: 214). Recognising that social appearance rather than her happiness was the issue for friends who claimed to worry about her, Eliot also remarked sardonically, 'I cannot think that their digestion will be much hindered by anything that befals a person about whom they troubled themselves very little while she lived in privacy and loneliness' (*GEL* 8: 128). Eventually, Eliot even expressed a kind of triumph in her exile. In 1860, she informed a friend that when Lewes was told by a lawyer that he would not be able to secure a divorce (because he had allowed the first of his wife's illegitimate children to take his name and so was presumed to condone the adultery), she did not feel sorry: 'I think the boys will not suffer, and for myself I prefer excommunication' (*GEL* 3: 366).

Eliot was not without friends during the trying first years of her exile, however, and some of these were women who risked their own reputations in order to support Eliot and Lewes. Even before she left for Germany, Eliot consulted two close friends, Barbara Bodichon and Bessie Parkes, about the decision. Rufa Hennell, Sara Hennell and Cara Bray learned about the Lewes relationship only after Eliot had departed for Europe, but they eventually came round to accepting the situation, and their friendship with her lasted until her death. Rufa, in fact, was the first woman to visit Eliot after she returned from her European trip. Bessie was the second – a gesture that was especially courageous, since her father had forbidden her even to communicate with her old friend. Eliot also formed intense friendships over the years with many other women, and her letters to a number of them, in a long tradition of female letter-writing, used the language of marriage and love to describe her feelings about these relationships. Richard Ellmann diagnoses this epistolary style not as a genuine expression of affection on Eliot's part, but as evidence in her of 'a superabundance of amorous sentiment, beyond any immediate object'[14] – a version of Haight's theory about Eliot's excessive emotionalism.

Ellmann's and Haight's analyses are not uncommon: in patriarchy, love between women exists as a kind of black-market that functions outside the sexual economy; for this reason, Eliot's feelings for persons of her own sex need to be explained away as testimony of her 'emotional precipitancy'. A disinclination to acknowledge any affection even approaching lesbianism underlies many of these explanations. Haight, for example, tries to gloss the relationship with Edith Simcox – a woman who made no secret of the fact that she was in love with Eliot and whom Eliot treated with great kindness – by using a *non sequitur* typical of patriarchal attitudes toward love between women: 'Despite her rather heavy features, there was nothing masculine about George Eliot'.[15] Haight also exhibits some discomfort, on account of its intensity, in writing about Eliot's correspondence with Elma Fraser Stuart – a reaction he does not have to the excessive emotionalism of Alexander Main, whom John Blackwood called 'the Gusher' because of the uncontrolled adulation in his letters to Eliot. Biographers had found no difficulty in finding a place for male adoration of Eliot; her attachments to women, however, and theirs to her, have continually been presented as problematic.

It was during the time of isolation following her return to England that Eliot first began to write fiction with a view to publication. That she was thinking about the implications of such a decision is obvious even in her journalism, much of which dealt directly or indirectly with the difficulties faced by an intellectual woman. Taking advantage of the anonymity that was standard in nineteenth-century journalism, Eliot assumed the authority of a male voice while making hard-hitting points about the position of women within patriarchy – and within the professional establishment of writers. In her 'Art and Belles Lettres' column for the 1856 *Westminster*, for example, she pointed out – in a male voice – that as many 'silly *men*' as silly women were rushing into print and that it was good for men to take up the traditionally feminine task of writing children's stories. In 'Love in the Drama', Eliot used the journalistic male voice to analyse in unusually candid terms the repression of female desire in patriarchal culture. Contrasting with 'Walter Scott's painfully discreet young ladies' those heroines from classical drama and from Shakespeare who openly declared their love to men, Eliot described the expression of female sexuality as 'a natural manifestation which has only been gradually and partially repressed by the complex influences of modern civilisation'. Another review quoted poetical excerpts from *Bhanavar the Beautiful* that are in fact lyrical expressions of female sexual desire. In 'Menander and Greek Comedy', Eliot speculated about the 'domestic ascendancy' of women in ancient Greece, and in 'Mary Wollstonecraft and Margaret Fuller' – in addition to bringing to light the much neglected Wollstonecraft – she explored the ways in which sexism leads to the debasement of men as well as of women. A review of Harriet Beecher Stowe's *Dred* ended with a plea common in Eliot's anonymous journalism for women's education, while 'Woman in France' praised salon culture in part for the way it equated friendship and love.[16] Eliot had also intended to write articles entitled 'Ideals of Womankind' and 'Woman in Germany', but Chapman rejected these ideas.

The most famous of Eliot's journalistic publications is

'Silly Novels by Lady Novelists', the article she wrote
less than two weeks before beginning her first story, 'The
Sad Fortunes of the Reverend Amos Barton'. Although
Eliot has been criticised as 'unsisterly' for her 'refusal to
acknowledge' in 'Silly Novels' that she was a woman,[17] the
essay reveals the complex double-voiced technique that
characterises her journalism and early fiction: using an
ostensibly male voice, Eliot could say what would not be
considered seriously were she recognised as a woman. In
the case of 'Silly Novels', which Eliot saw as a source of
'wholesome truth' and 'amusement' (*GEL* 2: 258), she was
thus able to criticise not only the women's fiction she re-
garded as second-rate, but also, more important, the literary
market in which a double standard that judged women and
men separately fostered mediocre feminine writing. The
essay is, on one level, a rumination on the particular difficulties facing a woman writer trying to be taken seriously
by a literary establishment that could not separate her
writing from its own condescending attitudes toward her
gender. Such biases were enforced by the convention in
most Victorian journals of devoting a single column in each
issue to the works of women writers – thus placing them in
competition only with each other and segregating them from
the mainstream masculine market. Eliot had already herself
been the victim of this literary double standard: her anonymous translation of Strauss had been praised as the work of
'a man who has a familiar knowledge of the whole subject',[18]
while her later translation of Ludwig Feuerbach's *The Ess-
ence of Christianity* – the only work ever to appear with the
name 'Marian Evans' on its title page – was flippantly
dismissed as the work of a 'lady-translator' (*GEL* 2: 187, n.
8). It is therefore understandable that Eliot felt uncomfortable at being mentioned 'in the character of Editress' to
Francis Newman – a man, she had been told, who had 'no
high esteem of woman's powers and functions' (*GEL* 2: 85)
– and that she wanted to keep secret the authorship of one

of her most serious review-essays ('Evangelical Teaching: Dr. Cumming') because its effect would be weakened if it were known to be written by 'a *woman*' (*GEL* 2: 218).

Nor is it surprising – precisely because she was concerned about its effect on her readers – that Eliot's first work of fiction should have a male character's name in its title and that it should be narrated in a male voice. Eliot did not immediately assume a male pseudonym, however. When she wrote 'The Sad Fortunes of the Reverend Amos Barton', Lewes, calling the writer his 'clerical friend' (*GEL* 2: 273), submitted it to John Blackwood. The story was then published anonymously, and only after widespread speculation about the sex of its author did its two successors, 'Mr. Gilfil's Love-Story' and 'Janet's Repentance', along with the bound collection of the three stories, *Scenes of Clerical Life* (1857–8), become associated with the name 'George Eliot'. Eliot's choice of pseudonym has always been a subject for theorising about both her personal life and her attitude toward her writing. It has been suggested that the name offered Eliot a way of taking Lewes's name without formally marrying him and that it expressed her redefinition of the marriage tie.[19] Those seeking more literary reasons for the name have seen connections with Anne Elliott of Jane Austen's *Persuasion*, with the name Jane Eyre assumed during her exile, and with the fiction and personal life of George Sand – who herself had taken as a pseudonym her lover's name.[20] Others have offered psychological interpretations. Alexander Welsh, for example, explains the 'true secret' of Eliot's pseudonym as 'the ordinary concealment of writer from reader'. Welsh downplays the issue of gender, in spite of the fact that women had a peculiar susceptibility to the shame he associates with blackmail and with the self-protectiveness of all writers. Some feminist critics, however, have taken seriously the factor of gender when analysing George Eliot's assumption of a masculine pseudonym: Showalter sees it as a strategy to fulfil a female fantasy of

escaping patriarchal judgements, while Mary Jacobus inter-
prets the name as the expression both of Eliot's self-hatred
and of her ambivalence toward her position as a woman
writer.[21] One still cannot avoid the crudely practical reasons
for Eliot's transvestism, however, which are starkly dramatised in the reception of her early works of fiction.

The publication of *Scenes of Clerical Life* inspired many
theories about its authorship – the most common of these,
held even by Blackwood at the outset, being that it was the
work of a cleric from the provinces. Only Charles Dickens
openly speculated that the text was by a woman (Jane Carlyle
thought the author was a man who had been influenced by
his wife). More troubling for Eliot than these theories,
however, was the widely spread rumour – based initially on
the fact that some of the book's characters were recognised
as based on actual people from the part of Warwickshire
where Eliot grew up – that *Scenes* was written by a destitute
local cleric named Liggins who had not even been paid by
Blackwood for his labours. When Eliot published *Adam
Bede* in 1859, therefore, she was tempted to reveal her
identity (as she finally had, some time before, to Blackwood). She knew, however, that the book's reputation
could suffer on account of such a revelation – both because
her illicit association with Lewes was widely known and
because she was a woman. The reviews of Charlotte
Brontë's *Jane Eyre*, published twelve years earlier, which
had changed radically in tone when her identity was discovered, had demonstrated the danger of allowing a serious
fictional work to be judged by the standards Eliot had described in 'Silly Novels'. Lewes himself had written a
gender-biased review of *Jane Eyre*, and in 1849 Brontë had
written a bitter letter to him about it. Perhaps because she
was aware of Brontë's example, Eliot decided to keep her
identity secret – even from most of her friends – until after
Adam Bede had been reviewed.

The results of this strategy were predictable. Before Eliot

revealed herself, *Adam Bede* was widely praised, often for its masculine traits. A review in the *Economist*, for example, singled the novel out for its difference from feminine fiction,[22] and the *Eclectic Review* pronounced it the work of a 'brave, manly soul'. After Eliot had dropped her masculine veil, however, *Adam Bede* was suddenly analysed in terms of all the standard assumptions about female authorship. The *Athenaeum* suggested in its weekly gossip column that the Liggins rumour had been a feminine 'trick' or 'mystification' to promote *Adam Bede*. The *Examiner* associated the novel's 'melodrama' with its female authorship and complained about its depiction of 'the stages of childbirth, related with almost obstetric accuracy of detail'. The *Quarterly Review*, echoing the earlier social response to Eliot's disreputable marital status, attacked *Adam Bede* for the danger it presented to 'our young women in the middle and higher ranks' because it dealt with topics that fathers and brothers would not mention in a young woman's presence.[23]

Many people, in fact, expressed horror at learning that *Adam Bede* was by the same Marian Evans who had shocked London society a few years earlier. Henry Crabb Robinson – distressed that the 'translatress of Strauss' and 'a woman whose history is at least so unfortunate as Miss Evans's' could have written 'so admirable a book' – remarked, 'I would rather so excellent [?] a book was written by any man than a woman'.[24] And even Elizabeth Gaskell, who had briefly subscribed to the Liggins theory, expressed a similarly irrational wish that *Scenes* and *Adam Bede* had not been written by a woman with such a history – though she later overcame her initial 'moral' impulse to condemn Eliot (*GEL* 3: 226, n. 6). One of the most interesting theories about the authorship of *Adam Bede* came, however, from Anne Mozley, who, in an anonymous review published before Eliot's identity had been revealed, based her speculation that the novel was written by a woman on its unique perspective. Women, Mozley remarked, are 'the great clerical sympathisers' because 'the politics of a parish, its leaders and party divisions', are 'the most stirring bit of public life that comes under their immediate eye' (*Heritage* 90). This review, more than any other, crosses the essentialist boundaries of nineteenth-century reviews and sees the book according to an idea of gender as culturally produced.

The Mozley review might also be an unusually astute response to Eliot's use of the male pseudonym as a literary device exposing the very process of gender-coding that it seeks to escape. This aspect of the pseudonym is evident both in the exaggeratedly masculine pose of the narrator before Eliot's identity was revealed and in the persistent use of the masculine name after Eliot was known to be a 'lady novelist'. The continued assumption of the male voice could achieve for Eliot, as Gillian Beer has interestingly suggested, a reworking of the masculine name 'into the form of the woman's body, the woman writing'.[25] Neither male 'master' nor silly lady novelist, Eliot established by her pseudonym her difference from the gendered categories assumed by nineteenth-century reviewers and readers.

To assert difference was not to escape the old assumptions, however, as the reception of Eliot's next novel, *The Mill on the Floss* (1860), amply demonstrates. Eliot daringly focused this work on the repression of a young girl by patriarchal gender codes, and she was punished for this by the reviewers, who now knew without doubt the gender of 'George Eliot': the novel was not received with nearly the enthusiasm that *Adam Bede* had attracted before Eliot lifted the masculine veil. Her reputation was partly protected, however, by the history of her first two works: no one could take back what had been said about them before they were known to be written by a lady novelist. A new strategy therefore emerged in the reviews: the greatness of Eliot's fiction was not denied, but she was compared chiefly with female writers and was championed, by those who praised her, as the greatest *woman* writer. This segregation and tokenism served the double purpose of containing at once Eliot's reputation and those of her female contemporaries, who, as Showalter has pointed out, were 'forced into secondary status' in relation to Eliot.[26]

This condescension and containment persisted throughout Eliot's literary career – in spite of the fact that she was more productive than many of her male contemporaries. She also experimented continually in new genres; often, she alternated between writing a traditional provincial novel and working in a new form. After the appearances in 1859 of a short story entitled 'The Lifted Veil' and *The Mill on the Floss*, she began work on a historical novel set in Renaissance Florence, took time off from that work to write *Silas Marner* (published in 1861), then returned to the earlier project, publishing it under the title *Romola* in 1863. During 1864, Eliot began work on a play, originally conceived as a dramatic vehicle for her friend, the actress Helen Faucit. Again, however, she was sidetracked from that work and wrote another novel, *Felix Holt, the Radical*, published in 1866. She then returned to her play and published *The Spanish Gypsy*, a drama in verse, in 1868. During these years, Eliot had also begun to write shorter poems, many of them narrative.

In 1869, Eliot began work on her most ambitious project to date, the novel that eventually was published under the title *Middlemarch*. This task was interrupted, however, by a serious family crisis. During the years when Eliot had worked as an established novelist, her life had been divided between time spent in England, where she did much of her writing, and her trips to the Continent, during which she and Lewes researched their separate projects and generally recouped their energies. Their lives were complicated, however, by the responsibility of Lewes's three sons, who came to regard Eliot as a loving stepmother – their 'Mutter'. When they were boys, Lewes's sons were sent to boarding schools, but as they approached the time when they had to fend for themselves, it became necessary for Eliot and Lewes to take them in and to live in London, where employment for middle-class young men was easier to find than in the country. Charles, the eldest son, eventually secured a position in the Post Office and married in 1865. The two younger sons, however, had some difficulty in making careers for themselves and eventually took advantage of the British imperialist presence in Africa by buying farmland in Natal. Then, in May of 1869, the middle son Thornton arrived back at Eliot's and Lewes's house, suffering from a serious spinal condition that killed him the following October. During the intervening months, Eliot spent much of her time by her stepson's bedside, and he died in her arms. When the youngest son, Herbert, died in Natal in 1875 (perhaps of the same disease), Eliot and Lewes undertook to support his widow and children. Though Eliot had made the decision not to bear children of her own, she fully assumed the role of stepmother to Lewes's sons (as well as their wives and children), loving them as if they had been her own.

Eliot's maternal feelings were directed not only toward her stepsons, but also toward many of her friends – and she did not regard this adoptive motherhood as an inferior substitute for biological maternity. As she wrote with unusual frankness to one friend in 1869, 'in proportion as I profoundly rejoice that I never brought a child into the world, I am conscious of having an unused stock of motherly tenderness, which sometimes overflows, but not without discrimination' (*GEL* 5: 52). Eliot directed this maternal affection toward friends of both sexes; 'getting older,' she remarked, 'brings some new satisfactions, and among these I find the growth of a maternal feeling towards both men and women who are much younger than myself' (*GEL* 5: 5). Interestingly, Eliot also invoked motherly feelings to describe her relationship both to writing, which she compared to pregnancy (*GEL* 8: 383), and to her books, which she continually called her children. Eliot's tone, however, was radically different from that of the critics quoted in Chapter 1, who used the maternal metaphor with reference to a female pathology. Eliot's use of the same image suggests, indeed, that her body – which she had so feared when her father died – had become, not a mediating object in a masculine exchange, but an instrument by which her sensuality could be inscribed and circulated through 'children' whose fatherless origin lay outside the patriarchal sexual economy.

During and after Thornton Lewes's fatal illness, Eliot devoted her creative energies to poems, many of which were later published in *The Legend of Jubal and Other Poems* (1874), and to the ever-expanding *Middlemarch* project, which began its serial appearance in December 1871. By this point, she had become the much-lionised prophetic figure that many later critics were to resent and ridicule. This reputation was partly created by talk about the social Sunday afternoons that she and Lewes hosted as a means, without interfering too seriously with their own work, of entertaining friends and new acquaintances. The proliferation of gossip about the receptions led John Cross, in fact, to emphasise that they were only a small part of Eliot's life and that they did not have the almost religious importance often ascribed to them.[27] Whatever the afternoons meant to Eliot, however, they certainly became an important departure point for much of the mythologising – of both a praising and a mocking sort – that has continued to colour her personal and literary reputation. Many felt flattered to be invited to the receptions and enjoyed the contact with Eliot and Lewes, while others saw the occasions as requiring absurd and hollow worship (it was in accounts of the Sunday receptions that the sibyl and diva images first emerged). Charles Warren Stoddard's description of the gatherings is interesting for its combining of these two points of view. Having heard satirical accounts of the receptions, he was pleasantly surprised by what he perceived to be Eliot's warmth and kindness. What Stoddard did mock, however, was the group of Eliot worshippers who 'sat transfixed and gazed rapturously' upon her.[28] Thus the woman who had been exiled from society for her sexual indiscretions had become, thanks to her intellectual accomplishments, an object to be revered. The two positions, however, have something in common: a compelling need to set Eliot apart from other women. As Beer has shrewdly noted, seeing Eliot as exceptional and anomalous made it unnecessary 'to rethink the situation of all women'.[29]

After Eliot had published *Middlemarch*, she began working on another major project involving a topic at least as foreign to her experience as the fifteenth-century Italian setting of *Romola*: the history of Jewish religion and culture. In *Daniel Deronda*, published in 1876, Eliot combined the familiar British scenes of much of her provincial fiction with action and characters – like those of her historical novel and many of her poems – remote from familiar Victorian culture. She thus brought into contact the two heretofore separate strands of her writing. As her correspondence with Harriet Beecher Stowe reveals, Eliot's hope was to educate the xenophobic British public about a foreign culture in the way that she had seen Stowe educate the American public about Blacks (Eliot could have been more influenced by Stowe, however: references to Blacks in her letters are deeply racist). The attempt was a daring one, and, predictably, the Jewish sections of *Deronda* invited more opprobrium than Eliot had received in years. She did not have much time to worry about the novel's reception, however, for a few months after its publication had been completed, Lewes became severely ill. Though he recovered enough for both of them to return to their work for another two years, Lewes continued to be in pain much of the time and died of cancer in November 1878. One of his last acts had been to send Blackwood the manuscript for Eliot's final published work, a collection of essays – narrated by an explicitly male voice – entitled *Impressions of Theophrastus Such*.

Eliot's grief was so overwhelming that she did not attend the funeral and was not willing for months to see any of her friends. During that time, she completed Lewes's unfinished scientific project, the third volume of his *Problems of Life and Mind*, and established in Lewes's name a Studentship at Cambridge for which both female and male students were eligible. A number of critics have suggested, based on the single word 'Crisis' in her 1879 diary, that Eliot discovered after Lewes's death that he had been unfaithful to her. There is no evidence to support this theory, however, and Eliot's continued visits to the cemetery after the diary entry was made raise serious doubts about the inference. What is most interesting about the theory, in fact, is that critics should have leapt so automatically to this conclusion – to the exclusion of all other possible readings of the word 'Crisis'.

At the end of February 1879, Eliot finally consented to see her friend John Cross, a banker, who had lost his mother ten days after Lewes's death. The two were able to console each other, and Cross gave her financial advice. During the next year Eliot and Cross (who was more than twenty years her junior) continued to see each other, and they were married in May of 1880. It was a union that brought Eliot not only a new sexual partner, but also a new family, and she delighted especially in the acquisition through Cross of loving sisters. Eliot's decision, however, provoked as much astonishment and horror as her illicit relationship with Lewes had done more than twenty-five years earlier. Some fell back on theories of Eliot's feminine helplessness and saw Cross as her chivalrous rescuer. Many others – clinging to a myth of romantic love that Eliot's relationship with the married Lewes had effectively refuted – saw the marriage to Cross as a betrayal of Lewes. Eliot herself was sensitive to this thinking. Two weeks before she was married, she visited her friend Georgiana Burne-Jones, who remembered afterwards 'the weariness she expressed of the way in which wisdom was attributed to her. "I am so tired of being set on a pedestal and expected to vent wisdom – I am only a poor woman" was the meaning of what she said if not the exact phrase, as I think it was'.[30] Eliot's sentiments here pinpoint an issue that may have troubled many of her contemporaries: having contained Eliot and her reputation by isolating her from other women, Victorian society did not know how to accommodate her return to respectability. For Eliot, her relationships with Lewes and with Cross were both valid; for many of her contemporaries, each relationship invalidated the other: she was eating her cake and having it too.

One person who did not question Eliot's marriage to Cross, however, was her brother Isaac, who immediately sent Eliot a letter of congratulation. In his eyes, Eliot had not been vindicated by her solitary position after Lewes's death, but in finding a legitimate male sponsor for her sexuality, she had finally fulfilled her feminine fate and so could be restored to the position of docile sister. Eliot did not enjoy her respectability for very long, however, nor did she ever see Isaac again. After only seven months of marriage, she was taken ill after getting chilled at a concert and died unexpectedly on 22 December 1880. She was sixty-one years old. When she died, she had just begun plans for a novel, set in the Napoleonic era, which would have featured a witty female spy. Eliot also left unfinished a letter she had been writing to a woman whose brother-in-law had recently died, in which appear the last words she is known to have put on paper: 'a sister's affection' (*GEL* 7: 349).

The arrangements for Eliot's funeral repeated in minia-ture many of the contradictions of her life. Cross contacted a number of people about the possibility of burial in Poets' Corner at Westminster Abbey, but the idea was quickly squelched because Eliot had been, in T.H. Huxley's words, 'in notorious antagonism to Christian practice in regard to marriage, and Christian theory in regard to dogma' (quoted in *GE* 549). Eliot was buried, therefore, in unconsecrated ground near Lewes. Most of her obituaries, however, did not mention her long relationship with Lewes – except those that disapproved of it – nor did they generally allude to her influential translations of Strauss and Feuerbach. Many of them attributed her genius to masculine influences, especially that of Herbert Spencer.

Newspaper accounts of the funeral were also tailored along patriarchal lines: repeated allusions were made to the many distinguished men who attended the service, while in most reports no women were mentioned at all – though it is clear from the private reminiscences of Edith Simcox and others that many women were among the mourners. Simcox also recalled in her diary account that while she was awaiting the procession a child asked her, 'Was it the late George Eliot's wife was going to be buried?' As if to acknowledge the effective containment of Eliot by patriarchy implied in the child's innocent question, Simcox noted, 'I think I said Yes' (quoted in *GE* 550).

That Eliot had finally become a wife did, in fact, have an effect on the terms in which she was commemorated and remembered. Accounts of the funeral made prominent the fact that Isaac Evans, who was now willing to acknowledge in public the sister he had never spoken to during almost thirty years, was one of the chief mourners. Eliot's final place within patriarchy is perhaps best expressed in the words of her sister Fanny, who wrote to Isaac in 1881, 'We may be thankful that she had found a good husband and a *Name*, it comforts me to know that she who for so many years was believed to be the wife of Lewes, had not Mary Ann Evans inscribed on her coffin.'[31] To cite Irigaray again, Eliot had finally submitted to 'the monopolization of the proper name ... by father-men'.[32] And in the eyes of many like her sister, the patriarchal proper '*Name*' of 'Mary Ann Cross'

had indeed subsumed the succession of titles that expressed
Eliot's longstanding exclusion from and opposition to mas-
culine hegemony: 'Marian Evans', 'Marian Lewes' and
'George Eliot'.

In examining George Eliot's life in terms of her anomalous position within patriarchy, I have emphasised those
incidents and interpretations that would be most interesting
to a feminist reader. This does not mean, however, that I
see her as an example of the ideal feminist. There have long
been two opposing positions in the debate over Eliot's position in the feminist struggle, and in my view both tend to
distort the evidence. Those who try to mould Eliot into the
perfect feminist tend to omit, for example, that she was not
in favour of female suffrage and that she did not actively
participate in the feminist projects urged upon her even by
some of her closest friends. Those who try to cast Eliot as
opposed to feminism, on the other hand, tend to oversim-
plify her position. The most common accusation is that
Eliot did not grant to her fictional heroines the freedom and
adventure that she enjoyed herself. Neither of these views,
however, takes into account the complexity of Eliot's life. As
Deirdre David has pointed out, Eliot was both a saboteur
of, and a collaborator with, patriarchy: without sabotage,
she could not have become a writing woman; without col-
laboration, she could not have achieved professional success
in a masculine world.[33] The same contradictory qualities,
we shall see, inform Eliot's fiction.

3 *Scenes of Clerical Life* and *Adam Bede*: Fictions of Female Sacrifice

George Eliot's fictions, like her life, at once reflect, expose and undermine the hierarchical ideologies of patriarchy. Subversion was not necessarily a fully conscious strategy on Eliot's part, however. As Mary Poovey has noted, the female writer's responses to the restrictions that bind her can create in her work, even without her knowledge, contradictions that 'may emerge in the discrepancy between [her] explicit aesthetic program and the emotional affect the text generates'.[1] In Eliot's fiction, such incongruities appear most frequently in the self-subverting structure of her plots; in the exaggeratedly male or the ambivalently androgynous voices that tell her stories; and in the overdetermined position created for the reader by those plots and voices – a position that can lead the reader to supplement and to resist the text's apparent or explicit meaning. Often, Eliot's fictions elicit a double or a multiple reading, one which emerges from a radical disjunction between, on the one hand, the aims achieved by the conventional plot and voice and, on the other hand, the desire for a different story and treatment fostered by the narrative's detailed attention to the consequences of sexual difference in patriarchal culture: a 'gender plot' works against the grain of the conventional narrative of romantic love or personal development, exposing its privileging of the masculine.

This doubleness in Eliot's fiction makes her treatment of endings especially interesting and problematic. In even the

most traditional of her narrative structures, the gender plot
interferes most violently with the teleological thrust of the
narrative just at the point of conventional closure – at
precisely the moment when the reader has been led to
expect a neat resolution of the tensions within the text. This
collision of values in Eliot's endings often results from her
use of the Conclusion, Epilogue, or Finale: the very devices
that suggest an overdetermination of closure work to undo
the resolution they pretend to achieve. Such Penelope-like
unravelling of the plot even as it reaches closure is some-
times also the result of the juxtaposition of interlocking
plots in the narrative conclusion: the resolution of one or
more subplots can undermine the values that seem to be
bringing the main plot to its triumphant termination. Eliot's
texts thus reflect what Rachel Blau DuPlessis has described
as a basic characteristic of closure: 'Any resolution can have
traces of the conflicting materials that have been processed
within it. It is where subtexts and repressed discourses
can throw up one last flare of meaning'.[2] Conflict of meaning, interestingly enough, was something that Eliot once
half-comically associated with feminine writing. Toying
with the stereotype of woman as unstable and fickle, she
wrote to John Chapman in 1854, 'Your letter made me glad
and sorry. It is the immemorial fashion of lady letter-writers
to be glad and sorry in the same sentence, and after all, this
feminine style is the truest representation of life' (*GEL*
8: 115).

Scenes of Clerical Life, most of which was written before
even John Blackwood knew its author was a woman,
appears on the surface to have none of the doubleness of
'feminine style'. Narrated by an upper-class man who
reminisces about his past as a 'genteel' youth wearing tails
and coming home 'for the midsummer holidays' from a
'distant' school ('Janet's Repentance' 5), the stories explicitly
address upper-class masculine readers and single out for
scorn the 'feminine' reader – satirically called 'Mrs Farthin-

gale' – 'who prefers the ideal in fiction; to whom tragedy means ermine tippets, adultery, and murder; and comedy, the adventures of some personage who is quite a "character"' ('Amos Barton' 5). By assuming for the voice of her stories – as she had in her journalism – both the class and the gender that possessed power in Victorian patriarchy, Eliot could give to her narratives those trappings of authority that were denied to the female author. The same device, however, can also be read as calling into question the equation of authority with particular categories of class and gender – and also of race. More than a game of disguise, the assumption of the masculine voice can serve as a strategy to foreground the textual codes that construct difference itself.

This phenomenon is immediately apparent in 'Amos Barton', for example, where the narrator seems at points to have a fixed identity, but at other times manifests an unsettling doubleness as he is seen to suffer from the very weaknesses and marginality associated with the feminine. On the first page of the story, even before the reader has been given any information about the narrator's gender, he confesses that he lacks the basic trademark of Victorian masculinity, 'a well-regulated mind', and refers to the vulnerable time of his young childhood when his nurse smuggled bread-and-butter into church for him. When he finally reveals his gender at the beginning of Chapter 2, he does so by describing the way in which his own gaze – and the illusion of self-sufficiency that enables it – can be turned back on himself: 'Let me discover that the lovely Phoebe thinks my squint intolerable, and I shall never be able to fix her blandly with my disengaged eye again.' Here the 'disengaged eye' that envisions the woman as object is itself made a passive thing to be scrutinised and rejected. The masculine speaker is manipulated into the feminine position.

This continual shifting of narrative positions puts the reader into a state of radical dislocation, as she or he is continually confronted with new and contradictory ways of perceiving. Consider, for example, this description by the personalised male narrator, in which, even on the domestic subject of tea with cream, he claims a superior point of view:

> Reader! *did* you ever taste such a cup of tea as Miss Gibbs is this moment handing to Mr Pilgrim? . . . No – most likely you are a miserable town-bred reader. . . . You have a vague idea of a milch cow . . . and you know nothing of the sweet history of genuine cream, such as Miss Gibbs's: how it was this morning in the udders of the large sleek beasts, as they stood lowing a patient entreaty under the milking-shed; how it fell with a pleasant rhythm into Betty's pail, sending a delicious incense into the cool air; how it was carried into that temple of moist cleanliness, the dairy, where it quietly separated itself from the meaner elements of milk, and lay in mellowed whiteness, ready for the skimming-dish which transferred it to Miss Gibbs's glass cream-jug. If I am right in my conjecture, you are unacquainted with the highest possibilities of tea; and Mr Pilgrim, who is holding that cup in his hand, has an idea beyond you. (1)

Significantly – as if this scenario were a microcosmic view of patriarchal relationships – the *knowledge* or Platonic 'idea' of tea and cream is attributed only to Mr Pilgrim, though the cream is entirely the product of female labour as it moves from the cow to Betty's pail and then to Miss Gibbs's cream-pitcher. The cream, moreover, a product of a female animal, is itself presented as both contributing and transcending labour – in a double sense of the word – when it parthenogenically effects its class-conscious separation from the 'meaner' milk. Nor is the cream the only product of a hidden exploited work-force: the tea which accompanies it can come only from the colonised East, itself figured so frequently in the nineteenth century as dark female other-

ness (a contrast to the 'mellowed whiteness' of the cream).
The mixing of the tea with the cream enacts, in other words,
the imbrication of patriarchal and imperialist economies.
The narrator, however, does not recognise the participation
of the female bodies in the cream-making process or of the
colonised bodies in the growing and harvesting of tea, except as agents in a 'history' possessed by white upper-class
males. He thus turns the product of physical labour into a
sacramental object miraculously self-produced in its own
religious ritual, complete with incense and temple – with
Mr Pilgrim, presumably, as communicant or high priest.

The narrator's account subverts itself, however, for the
very exaggeratedness of his masculine pose draws attention
to its limitations, its exclusion of the mode of production
hidden behind Mr Pilgrim's afternoon refreshment. When
the narrator ignores the cow, Betty, Miss Gibbs, and the
colonised source of the tea, he indirectly invites the reader
to notice them. This device might be seen as a variation or
extension of what Luce Irigaray has described as feminine
'mimicry' – the deliberate assumption of the feminine role in
order to 'recover the place of [woman's] exploitation by
discourse'.[3] Here Eliot's narrator assumes the masculine
rather than the feminine role, but because of the hyperbolic
quality of the imitation, the result is similar: by his own
deficiencies, this speaker betrays the shortcomings of his
discourse and the extent to which his authoritative relationship to his version of 'history' is constituted only by this
same discourse, his costume of white upper-class maleness.
The male narrator also calls into question the convention of
omniscient narration: in a reversal of the usual narrative
structure – which begins with omniscience and then shifts
into character-bound focalisation – this personalised and
gendered speaker begins the story, but then at numerous
points lapses into the master discourse of omniscience, itself
more authoritatively masculine than any single incarnation
of maleness. In this way, omniscience, as well as the mimetic

illusion it is assumed to construct, is radically unsettled. The inhabitation of a male body and voice enacts both the processes that define the deconstructionist project: it simultaneously reverses and displaces the authoritative masculine voice.

A subversive subtext emerges in 'Amos Barton' not only in the subtle shifting of positions by its voice, but also in its plot, which relentlessly uncovers the patriarchal structures that govern life in the parish of Shepperton (even the workhouse has its 'pauper patriarch' [2]). Running in opposition to the plot of personal development that concentrates on the sad fate of Barton is the gender plot, which, in depicting the female support system that ministers to Barton, exposes the mediating position of women in the sexual economy. This is evident both in Milly Barton's apparently unnecessary death and in the narrative treatment of the lives of even the most minor characters, female and male. The story opens, for example, at the home of Mrs Patten, whose comfortable position exactly reverses that of the impoverished and continually pregnant Milly: originally a lady's maid, Mrs Patten is a 'childless old lady' who was 'married for her beauty' and who has 'got rich chiefly by the negative process of spending nothing' (1). In a sense, Mrs Patten has fulfilled the promise of her name, for pattens are footgear worn to keep one's feet above the mud.

Mrs Patten attributes her success in life quite literally to her shrewd moves in a commodity market that defines women as expendable employees. Significantly, however, she does not confer the benefits of her success on her unmarried fifty-year-old niece Janet Gibbs, who has refused offers of marriage 'out of devotion to her aged aunt' and who plays the role of servant for her (just as she hands the tea and cream to Mr Pilgrim, without herself being acknowledged). Janet is a reminder throughout the story of the limitations placed on the lives of 'old maids', women who have not found sponsors within patriarchy but who are enlisted, none the less, to serve it. Dependent on her aunt for support, Janet is forbidden by her even to go out on behalf of Barton's Track Society. A suppressed presence in Mrs Patten's home, Janet laughs at jokes told at her own expense and seems 'always to identify herself with her aunt's personality, holding her own under protest' (1). Thus the legacy of Mrs Patten's marriage and rise in class is the denial of opportunities to her niece: Janet's status as 'old maid' is constructed by her dominating aunt in order to bolster her own sense of superiority. Their relationship stands as a parodic version of patriarchal marriage: now that Mrs Patten is widowed, she assumes the masculine position toward her self-effacing and subservient unmarried niece.

The destructive Mrs Patten–Janet Gibbs relationship presents a useful framework through which to view the positions of the other women in the story. The Countess Czerlaski, for example, has managed through her complicity with patriarchy to accomplish only part of what Mrs Patten has achieved: by marrying a Polish count, she has risen significantly from her position as governess, but she has failed to acquire financial security commensurate with her new class. It is this failure that drives the Countess – after her brother has married her maid and thus duplicated the pattern of her own and Mrs Patten's marriages – to take advantage of Milly Barton, making her, in effect, a replacement for the lost maid, her own version of Miss Gibbs. Like Mrs Patten, too, the Countess is a 'man's woman': in spite of her 'careful elegance' when embracing Milly, she values only Amos's work and cultivates him in the hope that the association will bring her a new sponsor within patriarchy. When the plan fails, it is not surprising that the Countess should make things up with her brother, who can provide her with the supplementary income she has all along been seeking.

Both Mrs Patten and the Countess provide a sharp contrast with Milly Barton, the only wife in the story who has not made the best of her mediating position within patriarchy by marrying for money and class. Mrs Hackit's description of Milly serves as an alternative to Mrs Patten's commodity-based definition of a good wife, expressed in terms of an exchange of cheese for gowns (1). In contrast, Mrs Hackit expresses admiration for Milly because she works for no reward at all; both commodity and slave, she is Amos Barton's 'best treasure' (2). Presented in terms of 'imposing' grandeur, Milly plays an almost superhuman role in her marriage – taking on herself all the burdens of her husband's precarious financial and social position: while Amos eats with friends, drinks brandy, or sleeps, Milly ministers to him and their children, while endlessly mending the clothing that gives them the appearance of respectability. She also bears all the consequences of the sexual relationship with Amos, nurturing as well as giving birth to his children (the story hints that in addition to dying after the birth of her last child, Milly had also suffered a miscarriage during the previous spring). As Stephen Marcus has suggested, Milly dies as a direct result of her sexual intimacy with her husband.[4] Even Janet Gibbs does not envy Milly her position: 'if I was a wife', she remarks, 'nothing should induce me to bear what Mrs. Barton does' (6).

Amos, on the other hand, can enjoy – in spite of his poverty and unprepossessing character – the advantages of the patriarchal male, with outlets in the world of action and invitations to the homes of his wealthy neighbours. He is comfortable in the world of Parson Ely, who relishes keeping the women of Shepperton in a state of false hope about marital prospects with him, but whose real province is solitary 'bachelor enjoyment' (4) and the pleasure of playing generous host to his fellow clerics. Ely exemplifies the self-sufficiency granted to males within patriarchy – a contrast to the dismal isolation and dependence of Janet Gibbs. Amos, of course, is not so callous or conceited as

Ely, but he still passively represents masculine supremacy. Never actively hurtful toward his wife, like some of Eliot's later husbands, Amos nevertheless fails to notice when she is sick (his nine-year-old daughter does), nor does he show 'recognition of Milly's attentions' (2). When Milly is gravely ill before the birth of her child, it is Nanny the overworked servant, not Amos, who has the good sense to banish the Countess. Amos's strategies in chess – casually described by the narrator as those of players who 'create interesting vicissitudes . . . by taking long-meditated moves with their knights, and subsequently discovering that they have there-by exposed their queen' (3) – stand as a paradoxical paradigm for the story's structure: Amos bungles his moves, thus exposing Milly's queenly stature and simul-taneously destroying her; unlike the chess player, however, he does not lose the game when he loses his queen.

Nor is Milly the only woman who sacrifices herself to secure Amos's happiness. A constant though muted pre-sence in the story is that of the eldest Barton daughter, Patty, 'whose sweet fair face is already rather grave some-times, and who always wants to run up-stairs to save mamma's legs' (2). At her mother's deathbed, Patty – in a sublime version of Janet Gibbs's retreat from her own personality – identifies with her father's grief while restrain-ing her own, and unquestioningly accepts the maternal role conferred on her by her mother: 'Love your papa. Comfort him; and take care of your little brothers and sisters' (8). In fulfilment of this acceptance, Patty later appears as her mother's avatar, sitting at her father's feet, her head on his knee. The extent of Patty's sacrifice is most apparent, however, in the 'Conclusion', which seems superficially to be presenting a happy resolution to the sad story. Here Amos appears 'calm' and 'cheerful', and 'his neat linen [tells] of a woman's care'. Patty's own appearance, however, is not so free from trouble. She is described as 'a young woman' of 'about thirty', with 'some premature lines round

her mouth and eyes, which [tell] of early anxiety'. Patty's
position is then compared with those of the other children,
all of whom have 'gone their own several ways'. Her fate is
contrasted particularly with that of little Dickey, who has
grown into a 'man of talent' and with whom, our male
narrator reminds us – singling out for one last time the
story's implied male audience – 'you will be glad any day
to shake hands ... , for his own sake as well as his
mother's'.

The happy conclusion of 'Amos Barton' thus provides a
clear example of the doubleness that characterises Eliot's
texts. In terms of the plot suggested by the title, which
focuses on Amos's happiness, a satisfactory resolution has
been achieved. The cost of that resolution, however, is the
striking lack of such a happy conclusion to the gender plot,
which dramatises from beginning to end the differing fates
of its feminine and masculine characters. In spite of some
personal 'misfortunes', Amos and Dickey Barton – along
with all of the other incidental male figures – find some
fulfilment even after the death of Milly. Their happiness has
been created, however, by a female support system that
includes not only Patty Barton, but also, significantly,
Milly's unmarried aunt, Miss Jackson, who 'had withdrawn
herself, her furniture, and her yearly income' from the
Barton household after a 'slight "tiff" with the Rev. Amos'
(5), but who after Milly's death 'forgot old grievances' and
'came to stay some months . . ., bringing such material aid
as she could spare from her small income' (9).

In the world of 'Amos Barton', the happy fates of those
privileged by patriarchy – a complacent group that includes
Mrs Patten and the Countess, as well as the men – are
produced by the self-effacement of the women who serve
them: Milly Barton, Patty Barton, Miss Jackson and Miss
Gibbs. There seems to be a double meaning even in the
narrator's much-quoted declaration, 'A loving woman's
world lies within the four walls of her own home; and it is

only through her husband that she is in any electric communication with the world beyond' (7). These words describe
not only the selflessness of the loving woman, but also the
enormous restrictions that prevent her having any direct
contact with the 'world beyond' inhabited by men. The
passage also points up, by its failure to mention the single
woman, that she lacks even the 'electric communication'
provided by a husband to penetrate the four walls that
entrap her.

'Mr. Gilfil's Love-Story', a narrative whose title again
focuses on the fate of a male character, also discloses a
ruthlessly self-serving patriarchal economy, although here
the emphasis is on distinctions based on class and race as
well as on gender. Significantly, the narrator justifies his
account of Tina Sarti's life by dismissing the distorted and
incomplete memories of the already familiar Mrs Patten,
who typically is concerned only with the fate of Maynard
Gilfil's 'blood an' money' (1) – the transference of his
patriarchal assets (which, we later learn, he has inherited
from his mother). The narrator, in contrast, claims to be
'much better informed' than Mrs Patten and proceeds to
provide the background to her superficial memories by
telling a story that gives dignity to the rather ordinary Gilfil
and at the same time links his suffering to the tyrannical
influence of patriarchy.

The major force of masculine hegemony in 'Mr Gilfil' is
Sir Christopher Cheverel, whose gender, wealth and title
provide him with personal and political sway over his family
and associates. The entire plot revolves around the Baronet's
plans to create a successor to his fortune and position, plans
that are figured in his elaborate blueprint for a Gothic
renovation of his property (a parallel with Barton's plans to
renovate the church). Each character in the story has a place
in Sir Christopher's blueprint, and only death prevents the
perfect execution of his design. A minor figure in the
Baronet's plan is Tina Sarti, whose gender, poverty, lack of

title, and Italian nationality deprive her of the power to make a blueprint for her own life. Continually referred to by Sir Christopher as his 'little black-eyed monkey', Tina typifies the feminine position within patriarchy: ornament rather than agent, she can be passed from one man to another without regard for her own desires. Tina's power-lessness is made all the more dramatic, moreover, by the conditions of her 'adoption' by Sir Christopher and Lady Cheverel. Finding Tina orphaned at the age of three, they decide to take her in so as to cheer their house with the 'music' of a child's voice, but also to exercise their cultural imperialism: they consider it 'a Christian work to train this little Papist into a good Protestant, and graft as much English fruit as possible on the Italian stem'. The Cheverels do not intend, however, to replace Tina's lost cultural context with their own. They have no idea, we are told,

> of adopting her as their daughter, and giving her their own rank in life. They were much too English and aristocratic to think of anything so romantic. No! The child would be brought up at Cheverel Manor as a protegée, to be ultimately useful, perhaps, in sorting worsteds, keeping accounts, reading aloud, and otherwise supplying the place of spectacles when her ladyship's eyes should wax dim. (3)

As a child, Tina does not seem to suffer much from her subordinate status and indeed assumes the masculine posi-tion in her relationship with Maynard, who is compared with Samson and described as her 'slave'. Tina's power is dependent, however, on her having no sexual desire for Maynard. As the narrator explains, 'a passionate woman's love is always overshadowed by fear' (4). Tina's disentitle-ment, therefore, like Heathcliff's in *Wuthering Heights* (she also is a 'gypsy changeling' [2]), becomes most problematic as she approaches sexual maturity and discovers that her desires do not conform with her station in the class system and in patriarchy.

Tina's position differs from that of Heathcliff, however, on account of her gender: while he can mysteriously secure for himself the trappings of masculine power and can attempt to use money and property to carry out his revenge, she is left with no effective means to retaliate for the callous sexual manipulations of Anthony Wybrow, whose position as Sir Christopher's heir makes him feel as entitled to Tina's sexual favours as he is to the other objects in Cheverel Manor. Thus the dagger she takes from the armour-filled family gallery where Anthony has made love to her is a fitting weapon to turn against the future patriarch. It is also appropriate, however, that Tina should be prevented by Anthony's unexpected death from carrying out her planned revenge. As the narrator suggests by his comparisons of Tina to Helen, Dido, Desdemona and Juliet, she remains a victim of the patriarchal exchange of women, not its triumphant opponent. Her final revenge against patriarchy is achieved, therefore, by a passive retreat into death: the only escape from her status as object of exchange.

Nor is Tina's planned attack against the shallow and manipulative Anthony aimed directly at the source of her exploitation. As Anthony continually tells Tina, his courtship of Beatrice Assher is merely a 'duty' to his uncle, and self-protective though it is, this charge contains some truth, for Cheverel manipulates everyone according to his personal designs: he has chosen Anthony as heir because he wants to disinherit the son of his older sister, with whom he has fought; he has also selected Beatrice as Anthony's wife, in an act of displaced wish-fulfilment, because he had once wanted to marry her mother. Sir Christopher's treatment of his widowed tenant Mrs Hartopp may stand as a paradigm of his manipulativeness: refusing to give in to her eloquent request that he allow her to continue managing the farm her husband had rented, Sir Christopher arranges for her family to occupy a cottage with 'a bit of land' on which she might 'keep a cow and some pigs' (2) – hardly the farm she had hoped to keep but more than he had originally offered. By this means, Sir Christopher manages to maintain his patriarchal position: depriving women of power, he simultaneously makes them grateful to him and dependent on his paternalistic favours.

As a habitual benevolent despot, Sir Christopher has almost absolute power over those around him: his wife knows better than to cross him; Anthony is complicit with his plans in all things; Tina never ceases to fear – even after she has so obviously become a pawn in his patriarchal game – that she might displease him; and even Gilfil, who has more sense than any other character of what is happening to Tina, is continually protective of Sir Christopher's feelings and blames Anthony exclusively for her desperate unhappiness. Only Anthony's death – the discovery of which is ironically juxtaposed with a description of the Baronet gloating over the success of his plans – interferes with Sir Christopher's blueprint for the future. After this event, in his only moment of humility, the Baronet cries and declares, 'I didn't think anything would unman me in this way. . . . Perhaps I've been wrong in not forgiving my sister' (18). This single admission of guilt is actually the beginning, however, of the Baronet's retrenchment, for his regret at not forgiving his sister marks his intention to make her son his next heir. In this way, he can return, after a serious but not fatal interruption, to his plans for extending his empire into the next generation. Only temporarily 'unmanned', Sir Christopher appears at Tina's and Maynard's wedding – the carrying out of still another of his self-serving plans – secure again of an heir. His imposing presence at the marriage is dwelt upon by the narrator, who describes the admiration with which '"Mester" Ford, a true Staffordshire patriarch' (21), regards Sir Christopher. At this moment, closure seems complete, as Gilfil is finally rewarded for his patient love of Tina, while the family and community surrounding them are restored to their old hierarchical structures.

Significantly, however, the story does not end with this scene, but rather moves beyond the wedding – the standard closure of the romance plot – to provide the real basis for 'Mr. Gilfil's Love-Story': the loss that followed upon the seeming reconciliation of the marriage. This return in the conclusion to Gilfil's sadness – and its source in Tina's death – draws attention to the way in which subversion of patriarchy can lead to victimisation. Strange as it may seem, Tina – more than any other character – has acted as a challenge to Sir Christopher's plans. In spite of the fact that she was never able to test her impulse to kill Anthony, she was, without knowing it, responsible for his death by demanding that he explain his behaviour. As the narrator suggests, though Tina may never have stabbed Anthony, the 'fatal agitation' of his already weak heart 'was due to an appointed meeting with Caterina' (19).

Tina's second act of subversion – again an unconscious one – lies in her failure to make her marriage and motherhood, as both Sir Christopher and Gilfil have planned she should, the source of fulfilment. In spite of all the affection bestowed upon her, Tina dies of her pregnancy – the very solution that Gilfil had stubbornly hoped would obliterate her unhappy memories – and so refutes the easy patriarchal assumption that the biological experience of motherhood is an automatic solution to the damage done to women while they are being circulated in the sexual market-place. It is not Tina's foreignness that accounts for her failure to thrive, as some critics have suggested, but the exclusion and abuse that she suffers because of her gender, class and nationality.

The story's focus on Tina's Italian background (the original for her character was a British collier's daughter) serves to emphasise, in fact, not only the sexism but also the racism of Victorian culture. As such later works as *Romola* and *The Spanish Gypsy* also demonstrate, the use of a foreign context allows Eliot to present more extreme versions of bias and victimisation than the conventional plots of the 'provincial' fiction allow. Thus, although Tina is like Patty Barton in her readiness to adapt the posture of the docile child by sitting at Sir Christopher's feet, she does not possess even the limited privileges of a daughter. The Baronet prizes her only in the condescending and exploitative way he values the Gothic designs he has taken from Italy: holding Italians in contempt – he refers to his worker Francesco as 'a sad lazy dog' (2) – he plunders their culture for the decorations it can add to his estate. And just as Tina's nationality is the basis for her exclusion from the culture that has appropriated her, so it can be used – like the medical discourse about hysteria – as a rationalisation for 'her rebellion against her destiny' (2). Anthony explains to Beatrice, 'With that Italian blood of hers, there's no knowing how she may take what one says. She's a fierce little thing, though she seems so quiet generally' (12). Even Lady Assher's supposed compliment – 'All Italians sing so beautifully' (5) – is an insistence that Tina's expressions of pain are mere manifestations of hot Mediterranean blood. In these terms, the narrator's comparison of Tina's 'terrible struggles' with the 'conflicting thoughts and passions' leading up to the French Revolution is hardly hyperbole: Tina's position in Cheverel Manor, as her plan to stab Anthony makes clear, represents the kind of oppression that leads to violent action.

Tina's alliance with the labouring classes is evident in her relationships with the substitute parents she finds among the family servants. She values her former nursery maid Dorcas over the cold Lady Cheverel and goes to her as to a mother when she flees the manor after Anthony's death. And even in spite of Tina's fearful and guilt-ridden affection for Sir Christopher, it is to the 'nest' (7) of his gardener, Mr Bates, that she flees when she is displaced by the aristocratic

Beatrice. 'Uncle Bates' is not without his own biases, however, nor does he question the power structures that restrict both himself and Tina. He initially disapproves of Tina's 'adoption' by the Baronet and his wife, not because he anticipates the ways in which she will be excluded, but because he – as much as the others – distrusts her nationality. 'They're all alaike, them furriners,' he comments. 'It roons i' th' blood' (4). Nor can Bates fully understand Tina's predicament even after he has himself become a kind of adoptive father to her. When she flees to him, she finds that Bates himself – who in spite of his class is still free to exercise the appropriating male gaze – can speak of nothing but Miss Assher's beauty.

Although he never shares Bates's assumptions about the superiority of the British aristocracy, even the benevolent and maternal Gilfil is partly responsible for Tina's final fate because he has helped to implement the 'cure' that neglected the source of her disease. Tina's sexual response to Gilfil is no more impassioned than Hetty Sorrel's to Adam Bede after her rejection by Arthur Donnithorne, and the marriage seems just as inappropriate as one between Adam and Hetty would have been. This is apparent even in Tina's passive and childlike submission to Gilfil's sexual attentions, which is similar to Hetty's response to Adam, where Hetty is seen to 'put up her round cheek against his, like a kitten' (*Adam Bede* 34). As Tina begins to sing and then to cry for the first time since her illness, 'Maynard could not help hurrying towards her, putting his arm round her, and leaning down to kiss her hair. She nestled to him, and put up her little mouth to be kissed' (20). Hardly proof, as Knoepflmacher makes it, that 'Sir Christopher's decorative song-bird has become a woman at last',[5] this passage suggests that Tina's victimisation has disabled her permanently, leaving her the helpless child that Sir Christopher has always assumed her to be. The pathos of 'Mr. Gilfil's Love-Story' is not simply that Maynard has lost the woman he loved, but that even when they were married, her considerable vitality and passion – suggested so strongly by her haunting voice – were already severely damaged by her powerless position. Gilfil himself, moreover, who during Miss Assher's visit had given a sermon on the wise and foolish virgins – a text that foregrounds the idea of woman as commodity – has been a participant in this destructive process. His very adoration of Tina, imaged in the pathetic room that has become a shrine to her memory, can be seen as part of the process by which her desires have been suppressed. It is worth noting that Mrs Patten's account of how Gilfil used to look at Tina 'as if he was worshippin' her' had originally read in the manuscript, 'as if he could eat her'.[6] These two versions of Gilfil's attitude to Tina reveal the close relationship between the adulation and the consumption of women.

Thus Gilfil's unhappiness, privileged over Tina's in the story's title, is exposed as inextricably linked with her problematic position within patriarchy. The emotionally handicapped Gilfil, described at the end of the story as a 'poor lopped oak' that had been 'sketched out by nature as a noble tree' ('Epilogue'), seems finally just a male counterpart of the pathetically disabled Tina, who after her illness was compared to a 'delicate-tendrilled plant' that 'must have something to cling to' (20). Gilfil can thus be seen – as is suggested by the image in the first chapter of his masculine spurs pulling at his clerical 'skirts' – as still another image of doubleness in Eliot's narratives: a patriarch himself in his money, title, gender and position in life – like Sir Christopher, Gilfil makes a nephew his heir – he is simultaneously one more victim of a culture that represses and denies feminine desire.

While the first two stories in *Scenes of Clerical Life* concentrate on males who only passively or indirectly exercise their masculine hegemony, 'Janet's Repentance' – whose first word is the aggressive 'No!' of Robert Dempster

– depicts the most overtly violent man in all of Eliot's fiction. As if responding to the disturbing content of this story, Eliot's narrator is more forthright here than in the earlier stories in his acknowledgement of feminine victim-isation. Rejecting the views of those, like Miss Phipps and Mamsy Dempster, who assume that Janet Dempster is responsible for her own abuse, he asserts in no uncertain terms that Dempster's aggression is unprovoked and that it has been encouraged by the legal powers given to him in the marriage contract (13). Repeatedly, he draws the reader's attention to Janet's threatened position as Dempster's wife. Despite the narrator's pronouncements, however, contem-porary criticism of 'Janet's Repentance' tended to object, not to the characterisation of Dempster as an alcoholic and a brutal husband, but to the more serious violation of Victorian values, Janet's drinking. Eliot complained to one friend that Janet was 'the least popular of my characters' and that few shared her own 'satisfaction in Janet' (*GEL* 3: 35). Eliot defended the extremity of the story's violence to John Blackwood:

> The real town was more vicious than my Milby; the real Dempster was far more disgusting than mine; the real Janet alas! had a far sadder end than mine. . . . There is nothing to be done with the story, but either to let Dempster and Janet and the rest be as I *see* them, or to renounce it as too painful. (*GEL* 2: 347–8)

Blackwood and others were uncomfortable not only with the brutality presented in 'Janet's Repentance' but also with the lengthy opening chapters on Milby life. Eliot insisted on retaining these sections, however, because, she claimed, their relevance would 'become clear as the story proceeds' (*GEL* 2: 353). Eliot may have been referring here to the way in which the public and private spheres of the story run parallel and are linked by the actions of Dempster, whose aggressiveness is the basis for both plots: just as he beats Janet into submission, so he uses his professional power and influence to suppress Mr Tryan, the evangelical minister who plans to give Sunday-evening lectures in the church. In both cases, Dempster is holding at bay a feminine threat, for as the conversation at the Red Lion reveals, Tryan is seen by the men opposing him as a challenge to the masculine bourgeois hegemony that has empowered them. In their view, he is the instrument by which both women and poor people might gain ascendancy. The wealthy miller Mr Tomlinson – himself uneducated – complains, for example, that the lectures will merely 'brew mischief':

> There's work enough with the servant-maids as it is – such as I never heared the like of in my mother's time, and it's all along o' your schooling and newfangled plans. Give me a servant as can nayther read nor write, I say, and doesn't know the year o' the Lord as she was born in. (1)

The vehemence of Dempster's opposition to Tryan is similarly based in a fear of 'innovation' (2): he complains that the minister is 'perverting the faith of our wives and daughters' (4) and accuses him of 'praying with old women, and singing with charity children' in order eventually to take the position of Mr Crewe, the Anglican minister (1), and thus to destabilise the power structure that has given Dempster such influence.

The competitiveness of this masculine power structure is carefully portrayed in the Red Lion scene, in which Dempster and Pittman are seen as getting legal business because they are perceived to be unscrupulous, while Pratt and Pilgrim are described as driving away all competing doctors from their professional territory. In this Darwinian struggle for survival, Dempster uses sheer bravado and intimidation to discredit Luke Byles's correct point about the etymology of the word 'Presbyterian'. In the masculine worlds of the Red Lion and of professional Milby, aggression alone – exactly the instrument that Tryan does not use – determines the financial, political, and social hierarchy. It is not surprising, therefore, that Tryan should be perceived as a special threat when he begins to attract the interest of 'one or two men of substantial property' and 'a number of single ladies in the town' (2). To influence these people is, in Dempster's view, to '[infect]' both the wielders of power and the virginal currency which sustains the sexual economy.

Placed in direct opposition to the scenes of masculine power struggle in the Red Lion are those describing Mrs Linnet's 'feminine party', which meets on the outskirts of the impoverished Paddiford Common (where Tryan lives) in order to start a Lending Library to make evangelical literature available to the poor. Presented chiefly in comic terms, this feminine world is not an arena for games of political power. The narrator describes these women, in fact, entirely in terms of their status as potential commodities in the marriage market. He classifies them as different types of 'old maids', depending on their age and desirability in the exchange of virginal females: Mary Linnet's market value is evident in the extensive 'fancy-work' spread out over her mother's parlour, while she defensively claims she is determined not to marry 'without a prospect of happiness'; Rebecca Linnet, though her mother's favourite, is a less attractive commodity than Mary, both because she does not do 'fancy-work' and because she is fat; Miss Pratt is the least marketable of all the women on account of both her age and her status as 'the one blue-stocking of Milby' who had 'occasionally dabbl[ed] a little in authorship, though it was understood that she had never put forth the full powers of her mind in print' (3). All of these women are contrasted with Miss Pratt's niece, who is young, beautiful and therefore still of value in the female commodity market.

Significantly, each of these women, even the still saleable

Eliza, is attracted to Edgar Tryan, and the narrator – in one of his more transparent expressions of the story's subversive subtext – seems to censor his own stereotypical response to this phenomenon:

> Poor women's hearts! Heaven forbid that I should laugh at you, and make cheap jests on your susceptibility towards the clerical sex, as if it had nothing deeper or more lovely in it than the mere vulgar angling for a husband. Even in these enlightened days, many a curate . . . is adored by a girl who has coarse brothers, or by a solitary woman who would like to be a helpmate in good works beyond her own means, simply because he seems to them the model of refinement and of public usefulness.
> (3)

Here the narrator addresses a woman very different from the consumer of sentimental fiction earlier satirised as Mrs Farthingale. Acknowledging the limitations placed on women in marriage, he shows an understanding of their yearning for a third gender that does not fall into the rigid categories of masculine and feminine. In these terms, the 'clerical sex', like the men of the Red Lion, is 'of public usefulness', but, unlike them, is refined, not 'coarse'. This hypothetical type of sexual partner stands in stark contrast with the subject of conversation among the women before Tryan's arrival: the tyrannical and violent Dempster, who abuses his wife. For the women of Milby, Edgar Tryan seems to offer the only possibility of finding a husband different from the men of the Red Lion. It is for this reason too that he is threatening to Milby's masculine power structure.

The action of 'Janet's Repentance' does not, however, accomplish the overturning of that structure. As its title suggests, the narrative focuses on a transformation in Janet Dempster, not in the culture that constructs both her victimisation and her 'repentance'. As David Carroll has suggestively remarked, Eliot's story is 'both a pastiche and a revision' of the conventional temperance novel. I cannot agree with Carroll, however, that the story's closure accomplishes a reconciliation in Janet between the opposite values of Dempster and Tryan.[7] What this 'revision' of the temperance novel seems to reveal, indeed, is the built-in limitations of such a plot structure: a woman's 'repentance' cannot erase the difficulties that led to her drinking in the first place, which include in this case not only the violence of Dempster but also the whole system that has fostered the Dempster marriage and put both Janet and Tryan in their respective positions of confessor and repentant sinner.

As in 'Amos Barton', incidental narrative details in 'Janet's Repentance' stand in unresolved tension with the value system that governs the story's closure. It is significant, first of all, that Janet's marriage to Dempster has as its background a series of dilemmas emerging from her position as a woman in Victorian patriarchy. The daughter of a widow who supported and educated her daughter by running a milliner's shop, Janet is drawn to Dempster because he represents an alternative to wasting away as a governess and because he is the only intellectual match for her in Milby (she is often castigated, in fact, for having exactly the type of mental quickness that has led to Dempster's success in life). Janet's mother, who initially disapproves of the union, is 'won over' to it 'by a foolish pride in having her daughter marry a professional man' (3). Mrs Raynor is then powerless after the marriage to help her daughter deal with Dempster's violence and can only cite the standard Victorian maxims that ultimately enforce woman's oppression: 'we must submit; we must be thankful for the gift of life' (14).

It should be noted, too, that Janet did not marry Dempster merely to rescue herself from the 'old maidism' so graphically described by the narrator. Janet has nostalgic memories of those 'too short years of love' when she and Dempster 'sat on the grass together, and he laid scarlet poppies on her black hair, and called her his gypsy queen' (24). This romantic background to the violent Dempster marriage serves to emphasise, in fact, the strong connection between the position of woman as romantic object and as object of abuse: in both cases, she is the passive focus for male projection and aggression. As Tina Sarti's predicament has already dramatised, moreover, to be a 'gypsy' is to play the role of a feminine other that must be repressed. In another sense, Janet's problems recall those of Milly Barton, for when Janet leaves Dempster's clothing on the floor, she feels 'as if she had defied a wild beast within the four walls of his den, and he was crouching backward in preparation for his deadly spring' (14). Here the narrator introduces a sinister variation on his description in 'Amos Barton' of the loving woman's world as defined by the 'four walls' of her husband's home: when the husband is cruel, the 'four walls' enclose not merely a prison, but also a place of danger. The image of four walls blocking out the surrounding world appears again in a more positive light after Dempster has himself become injured and so has lost the physical strength to harm Janet. The loving wife is restored, it seems, to a benevolent enclosure of 'four walls where the stir and glare of the world are shut out' and 'where a human being lies prostrate, thrown on the tender mercies of his fellow' (24). Even the sickroom, however, is not free of violence: it is within these four walls that Dempster's delirium takes the romantic myth to its logical end by transforming the 'gypsy queen' into a vengeful Medusa. In this last of his projections on to Janet, Dempster simultaneously recognises her victimisation and makes of her a version of his own destructive self. Inscribed within the conventional plot of the temperance novel is Eliot's powerful indictment of the standard plot of romantic love.

Even within the temperance plot itself, moreover, lies a subplot that diminishes the importance of the 'repentance' resolution: the virtue of Edgar Tryan, we learn, is as dependent on female sacrifice as is Amos Barton's contentment or Robert Dempster's cruel tyranny. Tryan's situation invites striking comparisons, in fact, with both 'Amos Barton' and 'Mr. Gilfil's Love-Story'. Like the successful Dickey Barton, who can pursue his professional career because Patty is caring for Amos, Tryan leaves the job of caring for his paralysed father to his unmarried sister. Her role parallels that of many other women throughout *Scenes* who manage the domestic world in order to give their husbands and brothers a place in the public sphere (this includes the author Miss Pratt, who for many years cared for her widowed brother's household). Even more ironic than the implicit similarity between Tryan and the Barton men, however, is the parallel between him and Anthony Wybrow, for both take advantage of their class and their gender to possess and discard a woman's sexuality. Standing in radical contrast to Janet's 'repentance' of her drinking, we learn, is Tryan's much more significant repentance of his sinful past. The reader's sense of Tryan's virtue is diminished, in fact, by his allusion to his responsibility for the death of a woman he had seduced as a reason for him to feel 'that I have been raised from *as low* a depth of sin and sorrow as that in which you [Janet] feel yourself to be' (italics mine): Janet's accountability for her drinking hardly equals that of Tryan for Lucy's suicide, provoked by his abandonment of her after he had 'induced her to leave her father's house' (18).

As a number of critics have complained, the description of Tryan's discovery of Lucy's body is pure cliché:

The body of a woman, dressed in fine clothes, was lying against a door-step. Her head was bent on one side, and the long curls fallen over her cheek. A tremor seized me when I saw the hair: it was light chestnut – the colour of Lucy's. I knelt down and turned aside the hair; it was

Lucy – dead – with paint on her cheeks. I found out
afterwards that she had taken poison – that she was in the
power of a wicked woman – that the very clothes on her
back were not her own. (18)

The passage seems deliberately clichéd, however. With its
emphasis on fine clothes, long curls, painted cheeks, and
the power of a wicked woman, it appears, in fact, to be a
verbal imitation of the image – common in pre-Raphaelite
paintings – of the discovery of the fallen woman (see, for
example, George F. Watts's *Found Drowned* [1850] and
Dante Gabriel Rossetti's *Found* [begun in 1853]). The effect
of this device is to call up in a few sentences the associations
of guilt and victimisation that accompany the image of the
fallen woman in Victorian culture and thus to 'revise' the
temperance plot once again by exposing its intersection with
the formally separate seduction plot. The doubleness in the
conclusion of 'Janet's Repentance' results, then, from the
collision of these two plots: an unforgettable background to
the image of Janet 'almost breathless' and 'on her knees at
[Tryan's] feet' (27) – a visual echo of Patty at Barton's feet
and Tina at Sir Christopher's – is the highly charged image
of the dead Lucy. In all three of the *Scenes of Clerical Life*,
at the very heart of the plot's resolution is a female sacrifice
on the altar of patriarchy.

Adam Bede, the first work of fiction in which Eliot makes
use of the standard romance plot, with its ending in a happy
marriage, appears in structural terms to depart radically
from the narratives in *Scenes of Clerical Life*, all of which
reach a conclusion of only muted happiness. The novel
contains many echoes of the earlier stories, however, and
embodies in its closure a similar tension between the fulfilment of the conventional plot and a subversion of that
fulfilment by the female sacrifice that concludes the gender
plot. Indeed, the emphatically happy closure of *Adam Bede*

serves to remind the reader all the more strongly of the prices that have been paid so that the patriarchal power structure might be restored. As the seduction plot involving Hetty Sorrel gives way to the marriage plot involving Dinah Morris, the narrative line itself draws attention to the losses sustained by both women in order to give Adam Bede the central patriarchal position his name and the novel's title imply. Hetty and Dinah, initially contrasted, are linked more and more closely as the plot progresses, and eventually Dinah literally replaces the transported Hetty as the wife of Adam and the possessor of the trousseau prepared by Mrs Poyser. What this easy replacement points up is that patriarchal marriage is built on losses and exclusions that cannot be altogether hidden or forgotten in the forced dénouement of the romance plot: in the conclusion of *Adam Bede*, the absence of the punished Hetty and the submission of the silenced Dinah to patriarchal marriage (she had earlier sympathised with dogs because they could not speak) create a sense, not of resolution, but of radical asymmetry. The fulfilment of the romance plot places feminine desire firmly in the subordinate position, as passive object of a masculine desire that both defines and restricts it.

The problematic privileging of masculine desire is a function not only of the plot in *Adam Bede* but also of its narrative technique. Here the male narrator's shifts of position often involve an interrogation of his own already established point of view, especially his frequent exercising of the gaze. As in *Scenes*, this narrator addresses male readers – especially when alluding to women – in a tone of camaraderie, while reproaching 'lady' readers for their superficial or biased interpretations (the famous defence of Mr Irwine in Chapter 17 is at one point addressed explicitly to women readers). Again, as in *Scenes*, the male voice also disguises a subversive subtext, in this case by dissociating himself from the limited masculine perspective even as he represents it. This is established in the second chapter of

Adam Bede, where the 'elderly horseman', later revealed to be Colonel Townley, the Stoniton magistrate, arrives in Hayslope on the evening when Dinah is preaching on the Green. Hugh Witemeyer has described this figure as 'demonstrating the quality of perception that the reader must learn to apply to the world within the novel', and William Myers sees his allegedly objective point of view as protecting Dinah from charges of unwomanliness and hysteria.[8] The narrator, however, maintains a careful distance from this observer's point of view and even on occasion argues with it. Townley thinks that 'nature' did not intend Dinah to be a preacher, but the narrator disputes this essentialist notion: 'Perhaps he was one of those who think that nature has theatrical properties, and, with the considerate view of facilitating art and psychology, "makes up" her characters, so that there may be no mistake about them. *But Dinah began to speak*' (italics added). Here not only the narrator's ironic tone, but also the actual fact of Dinah's preaching, interrupts and discredits Townley's patriarchal assumption. It is significant, therefore, that when Townley reappears at the end of the novel, he exercises paternalistic benevolence by allowing Dinah to enter the prison, but is also part of the legal system that condemns Hetty to death.

What Townley epitomises, in fact, is not objectivity, but a standard patriarchal point of view. As an 'elderly' man in a position of authority, he stops in the rural village to 'have a look' at the Donnithorne property and then, with a similar inquisitive impulse, to indulge 'his curiosity to see the young female preacher'. His response to Adam, whom he mentally enlists to 'lick the French' (2), also reveals a habit of visual appropriation. In these terms, it is significant that the stranger, like the other men watching Dinah, finds himself 'chained . . . to the spot against his will' by the 'charm' not of her body but of her voice: the very sound that the stranger had thought would be unnatural neutralises and counters his gaze – fixing him in place just as the appropriating eye seeks to control the object it scrutinises.

Dinah herself is aware that she is exempt from the stultifying and dangerous effects of the male gaze. When Mr Irwine asks her, 'And you never feel any embarrassment from the sense of your youth – that you are a lovely young woman on whom men's eyes are fixed?' she replies that she is safe from such visual assault: 'I've preached to as rough ignorant people as can be in the villages about Snowfield – men that looked very hard and wild: but they never said an uncivil word to me, and often thanked me kindly as they made way for me to pass through the midst of them' (8). The idea of Dinah as a woman walking unscathed through danger recalls her biblical antecedent, who, however, suffered an opposite fate – one closer to that of Hetty. When the Dinah of Genesis was out walking by herself 'to see the daughters of the land' (Gen. 34: 1), she was raped, and her brothers took revenge for the violation of their only sister. As Lori Hope Lefkovitz has suggested, Eliot is using Dinah Morris 'to untangle a tradition that sees evil in any beautiful woman who goes out unprotected'.[9] Instead of hiding her body from the view of men, a strategy that ultimately keeps patriarchal structures in place, Dinah uses her voice to prevent their reducing her to an object.

In clear opposition to Dinah's strategy of deflecting the male eye is Hetty's unquestioning submission to its power, and the narrator continually presents her in exactly the way she envisions herself, that is, as an erotic object. In his first description of her, he focalises the desiring perspective of Arthur Donnithorne and at other points he identifies closely both with Arthur's fixation, in the style of a Petrarchan lover, on the parts of Hetty's face and body and with Adam's blind idealisation of her seeming innocence. The narrator's responses to Hetty are not confined to those of Arthur or Adam, however, for as the story progresses he is seen both to exercise and to interrogate his own gaze as he shifts from desiring fascination to censure, to condescension, to self-accusation, to paralysed fear. His recognition of the consequences of the gaze is most obvious in his treatment of Hetty's flight after she discovers she is pregnant with Donnithorne's child. Suddenly the narrator's condescending remarks about Hetty's triviality and sensuality become veiled accusations against his own sex. 'What will be the end?' he asks,

> the end of her objectless wandering, apart from all love, caring for human beings only through her pride, clinging to life only as the hunted wounded brute clings to it?
>
> God preserve you and me from being the beginners of such misery! (37)

Here the camaraderie that characterised the narrator's earlier addresses to his male readers has become a frightened admission of potential shared guilt. Both Hetty's failings and her suffering are seen as originating in her construction by masculine desire.

Another suggestion of the narrator's horror at and complicity in Hetty's fate can be seen in his comparison of her to 'that wondrous Medusa-face, with the passionate, passionless lips' (37). This image again suggests a problematic doubleness, for Medusa's story, usually seen in terms of the petrifying effect of her stare, also points to female victimisation. In fact, both common versions of the Medusa myth – which Eliot had commented on in a personal notebook as examples of woman's 'undeserved punishment' – involve the precarious position of woman as object of the gaze. In the first, which looks forward to Hetty's vanity and sense of competitiveness with other women, Medusa is transformed into a monster by Athena because she has 'dared to compare herself in beauty' to the goddess; in the second, which looks forward to Hetty's seduction, Medusa is raped by Poseidon in Athena's temple and punished by the goddess 'because she was powerless to punish the guilty god'. [10] The emphasis of Eliot's source (a book by Adolf Stahr) is on the differing power of gods and humans, but the difference between Medusa and her persecutors (both Poseidon and Athena) is more particularly determined by gender and class – exactly the elements that make Arthur seem to Hetty like a god. In Eliot's version of the Medusa story, the woman eventually dies, while her seducer, protected by his godlike status, is reabsorbed into the patriarchal structure. If Dinah deflects the male gaze with her voice, Hetty – its object and victim – finally answers it with a voiceless look that terrifies and paralyses.

The petrification brought on by contact with Medusa seems, indeed, to affect even the narrator himself, who turns away from Hetty's frightening face after her flight and returns to a series of addresses to a normative male reader – this time about the superiority of second love – and concludes his story with a shift from the seduction to the marriage plot. This is achieved, however, only by the creation of gaps that left Victorian readers yearning for a sequel to the novel concentrating on Hetty's fate (GEL 3: 184). Only in the confession scene with Dinah (the single person who looks at Hetty 'unobservant of all details' [15] and thus free of an invasive gaze) does Hetty speak again and tell her story. Still absent from the novel, however, are accounts of crucial junctures in her history: not only Arthur's actual seduction and the discovery of her pregnancy, but also what occurred at her meeting with Arthur in the prison, and, most important, the circumstances of her transportation and death. Without information about these events, referred to only obliquely by the narrator, the novel's happy closure is lame and incomplete. Hardly an image of fulfilment, it represents a retreat from issues the narrator cannot resolve.

Even in the last happy scenes of Adam Bede, there are strong suggestions of the cost incurred to achieve closure of the romance plot. An important focus of the final chapters is the restoration of the Poyser family to its former state of patriarchal stability, with Dinah conveniently replacing Hetty as the mediating link between Mr Poyser and Adam Bede (Poyser apologises to *Adam* after learning of Hetty's arrest, and Adam initiates his courtship of Dinah while seated in Poyser's three-cornered chair). Any satisfaction one might find in this union is undermined, however, by the rigid narrowness of the Poyser parents, who have from the beginning been implicated in Hetty's fate. Not unlike Tina Sarti, Hetty was brought as an orphan into her uncle's household, not as a full member of the family, but as 'a domestic help to her aunt, whose health since the birth of Totty had not been equal to more positive labour than the superintendence of servants and children' (9). (The same fate was not suffered by the orphaned Dinah, who was raised by her Aunt Judith as if she had been her own child.) It is not surprising, therefore, that Hetty should form a dislike for Totty, who so voraciously consumes exactly the maternal attentions that Hetty is deprived of.[11] For Hetty, like the servants Molly and Nancy, receives only verbal abuse from Mrs Poyser, who seems unable to transfer affection to children not her own. Mr Poyser, too (who betrays his militaristic patriarchal attitude in his reluctance to have peace with France because it will harm the economy), reveals himself to be less than a loving parent to Hetty. As Mason Harris has suggested, his refusal ever to see Hetty again after her arrest parallels Hetty's own rejection of her child.[12] Thus Hetty's infantile qualities are linked to the denial of her needs by the 'patriarchal' (9) Poysers: with no genuine affection coming from them, her dependence on the reassuring attention of the male gaze is all the more acute.

From this perspective, curious details in the description of the Poyser household seem appropriate. In Chapter 49, where the family is seen restored to happiness, their 'timid feminine' cows are shown being driven into the milking yard by an excited and aggressive male bulldog, and the animals are made fearful and confused by 'the tremendous crack of the waggoner's whip, the roar of his voice, and the booming thunder of the waggon'. The 'vicious yellow cow' which had kicked over a pail of milk (like Hetty, she has broken the rules governing female commodities) is seen undergoing the 'preventive punishment of having her hinder-legs strapped'. In the same scene, Totty is clutching a doll 'with no legs and a long skirt', which her brother later takes away 'with true brotherly sympathy, . . . amusing himself by turning Dolly's skirt over her bald head, and exhibiting her truncated body to the general scorn – an indignity which cut[s] Totty to the heart'. Buried in the texture of the pastoral description of Hall Farm, these references to intimidation, constriction and exposure reveal a repression of the feminine at the very basis of the Poyser family structure.

That this repression will be extended into Adam Bede's family is also subtly indicated, not only by Adam's patriarchal name and his close association with Martin Poyser, but also by the repeated references to his views, paralleling those of the Poysers, about women preaching (he is also quoted – in his old age and hence after the novel's happy closure – as attributing to women ignorance of 'math'matics and the natur o' things' [17]). It is established in the first chapter of the novel that Adam is against the practice, and although he tells Dinah when he proposes to her that he will allow her to continue it, he eventually – as if giving vent to the same fear of a feminine threat in Methodism as that felt by the men in the Red Lion – expresses strong support of the Conference decision to abolish female preaching. Significantly, Adam's view is different from that of Eliot's own uncle, who, in proposing to her aunt (the original of Dinah Morris), emphasised that her marriage would not interfere with her preaching and who joined the Arminian Method-

ists with her so that she could continue to preach after the
Conference had banned such activity for women (*GEL* 2:
503, 3: 175). In these terms, it is significant that Adam is the
only man whose 'dark penetrating glance' can create in
Dinah Hetty-like blushes and 'self-consciousness' (11). The
lack of self-consciousness that had deflected the invasive
gaze during her preaching is obliterated by Adam, whom
Dinah twice calls a 'patriarch' (8 and 30). It is fitting,
therefore, that the Epilogue of *Adam Bede* should focus not
only on the marriage of Adam and Dinah, but also on the
revival of the male friendship between Adam and his own
patron in the class system, Arthur Donnithorne: with this
reconciliation, the male power structure has been fully
restored.

The symmetry of this restoration is undermined, however, by the presence at the end of the novel of so many
supernumerary figures whose positions within the patriarchal structures of the Poyser and Bede families are tenuous
or incomplete. In all of these characters, female and male, a
repression of the feminine signals an absence or lack in their
lives, even as they form relationships and 'marriages' that
mirror patriarchal power structures. There is Bartle Massey,
whose misogyny disguises his own maternal attitude to
Adam and whose unspecified victimisation in the sexual
market-place has been revealed in the scene when he goes to
console Adam. There is 'quiet Mary Burge, the bridesmaid'
(55), whose future, like Patty Barton's, will be confined to
taking care of her ailing father. There is Mr Irwine, who has
forgone any sexual relationships in order to support his
maiden sisters and to act as submissive servant – rather like
Miss Gibbs in her 'marriage' to Mrs Patten – to his 'half-
masculine' patriarchal 'witch-mother' (5). There is Lisbeth
Bede, whose continuing position of powerlessness in relation to both her husband and her elder son finds expression
in her querulous and helpless female language. And there is
her own submissive servant, Seth Bede – in her view less

than 'half the man' his brother is (4) – who from the beginning had offered complete freedom to Dinah and who is made 'silent' by Adam on the 'standing subject of difference' between them, the issue of women preaching. Seth, in fact – like Mr Tryan without his guilty history – seems, as a man free from patriarchal assumptions, one possible incarnation of the 'clerical sex' that the narrator in *Scenes* had imagined. Seth's solitary presence at the end of *Adam Bede*, like that of the other characters whose desires remain unfulfilled, exposes the suppression that is required to maintain patriarchy. For the standard romance plot to work, Eliot's narrative reveals, supernumerary desires must be marginalised, the female voice that deflects the male gaze must be silenced, and the unjustly punished Medusa, with her anguished face, must be banished.

4 *The Mill on the Floss* to *Silas Marner*: Fictions of Desire for the Lost Mother

While *Adam Bede* at least superficially fulfils the requirements of its romance structure, a much more obvious and radical subversion of standard plots operates in Eliot's next novel, *The Mill on the Floss*, which in its early scenes falls clearly into the tradition of the *Bildungsroman*. As several critics have noted, Eliot's focus on a female as well as a male child fundamentally alters the conventional plot of personal development and vocation: while the *Bildungsroman* traces the process by which the boy discovers his professional role within patriarchy, in presenting the girl's quest for identity it can only expose her exclusion from the same power structure. A similar disjunction appears in the novel's framework of nostalgia, established in the first chapter where the narrator wakes from a dream-like trance to tell a remembered story: here the values of the past revered by both Maggie Tulliver and the narrator serve to suppress exactly those feminine desires that have been brought to the surface by the female *Bildungsroman*. The reader is thus presented with unsolvable problems in interpretation, acknowledged even by the narrator, who continually refers to the instability of meaning in language. He remarks at one point, 'we can so seldom declare what a thing is, except by saying it is something else' (2: 1), and at another, 'the lines and lights of the human countenance are like other symbols

– not always easy to read without a key' (3: 7). Maggie
herself tells Tom that words 'may mean several things –
almost every word does' (2: 1). In *The Mill on the Floss*, to
fasten on one 'meaning' is to repress and exclude the
contradictory meanings also inscribed in the text. The novel
is the site of a continual struggle between the masculine will
to power constructed by patriarchy and the desires it must
repress to maintain its hegemony.

The focus for this power struggle is the two children,
Maggie and Tom Tulliver, whose positions within their
family and society are overdetermined by their gender. Eliot
takes the patriarchal social world that had been depicted in
her earlier fictions and examines its influence, not only on
young adults in a courtship plot, but also on children in a
plot of personal development that goes back to the time
when gender roles are constructed for the human subject. In
these terms, it is significant that Maggie is first seen when
she is 'gone nine' – a year younger than Hetty Sorrel when
she was taken in by the Poysers: Maggie, who is depicted as
embodying the sexuality but not the triviality of Hetty, is
seen during exactly the phase of childhood that is a notice-
able gap in Hetty's past. Maggie's position in the Tulliver
household is, moreover, a variation of Hetty's anomalous
role in the Poyser family. Though she is not an orphan,
Maggie is, like both Hetty and Tina, less than a full family
member because of what patriarchy perceives to be her
deficiencies: while Hetty and Tina are kept subordinate on
account of their genetic difference from the families that
'adopt' them, Maggie is seen as a 'mistake of nature' (1: 2)
even in her biological family because she has inherited the
characteristics of her father rather than of her mother and so
has traits and desires running counter to those constructed
by her culture as feminine. Her brother Tom, on the other
hand, though he has the feminine 'pink-and-white' (1: 5)
complexion of his mother's family and lacks the allegedly
masculine skill of 'apprehending signs and abstractions'

(2: 4), remains able to fulfil his family's expectations for him. As Maggie says to Tom, 'you are a man, Tom, and have power, and can do something in the world' (5: 5).

Maggie's powerlessness is depicted first of all in her relationship with her parents. Her mother sees marriage entirely as an investment of virginal household goods in exchange for sons: when her husband goes bankrupt, she complains most volubly about the loss of the tablecloths marked with her maiden name which she had purchased with her own money and which were meant for Tom. To such a woman, a daughter like Maggie – who fails to duplicate her own appearance, passivity and obsession with the objects of domesticity – is a mystery and a burden. Wishing that the docile 'pink-and-white Lucy' were her own rather than her sister's child, she is embarrassed by Maggie's dark looks and by her wild behaviour, which she compares to that of a 'Bedlam creature' (1: 2). Maggie's failure to conform with the standards for a marketable bride thus also diminishes her mother's affection for her.

Maggie's father, on the other hand, expresses love for his 'little wench' and admires her cleverness, but his commitment to patriarchal values finally makes him see his unconventional daughter simply as one more source of puzzlement in a world he fears and demonises because he cannot control it. Tulliver's need for dominance is apparent not only in his irrational aggression against Wakem and other lawyers but also in his decision to marry 'a buxom wife conspicuously his inferior in intellect' (1: 3) and in his projections of his fears and aspirations on to his son: he 'eddicates' Tom so that he will not rob his father of his position at the mill and, at the same time, so that the boy will be able to stand in for his father in the 'cock-fight' of legal struggle. A logical extension of Tulliver's self-protective notion that sons should represent fathers without displacing them is his view that daughters are commodities in a male sexual economy. It is not surprising, therefore, that although he realises

Maggie would make a better lawyer than Tom, Tulliver merely translates this perception into a worry that her intelligence will be a disadvantage in the marriage market. Maggie's interests are sometimes, in fact, a direct challenge to her father's world-view. While he superstitiously attributes the success of lawyers to Old Harry, Maggie – anticipating the Medusa image twice used to describe her – relishes Defoe's *History of the Devil*, leaving her father in a state of 'petrifying wonder' at the way in which the very subject on to which his greatest fears are latched engages his daughter's intellect.

While Tulliver worries about the consequences of Maggie's intelligence, her brother Tom has such rigid notions about sexual difference that he cannot comprehend the idea of his sister thinking. In Tom's view (as in the view of Mr Stelling), Maggie is by definition inferior to himself, and no evidence of her quickness alters his 'contemptuous conception of a girl' (1: 10). When they are children, Tom wields power over Maggie by establishing a relationship in which his acts of generosity can be matched only by her omissions and offences – a strategy he is able to carry out because of his more privileged status as a boy. Even the humiliating ex-perience of Mr Stelling's school, which temporarily puts Tom in the powerless position of a girl, does not alter his need – which matches that of his father – to master all challenges to his masculinity (even the cocks at his uncle's farm) and to dominate women. Tom's attitude toward Maggie thus combines those of patriarchal father and husband. The narrator's comment that the childish Tom 'was very fond of his sister, and meant always to take care of her, make her his housekeeper, and punish her when she did wrong' (1: 5) is later translated into his adult promise to Maggie – 'I shall always take care of you. But you must mind what I say' (3: 5) – and into his notion of patriarchal benevolence, which excludes any consideration of her de-sires: 'my kindness can only be directed by what I believe to

be good for you' (6: 4). It is natural, then, that when Maggie
fails to obey Tom, his rejection of her should invoke the
language of ownership: 'I wash my hands of you for ever.
You don't belong to me' (7: 1).

Raised in a family that adheres so strictly to patriarchal
notions about gender difference, Maggie is continually
confronted by her own conflicting desires. Her response is
intermittently to punish and to solace herself, just as she
comforts her legless trunk of a doll (Totty's doll without its
skirt – both emblems of female exposure and powerlessness) after driving nails into its head. Conflicting impulses
are similarly at work when Maggie forms relationships with
men. Her friendship with Philip Wakem is based both on
her sympathy for the feminine position imposed upon him
by his physical deformity and on her voracious appetite for
the intellectual pleasures he can bring her through his
contact with 'masculine wisdom' – 'that knowledge which
[makes] men contented, and even glad to live' (4: 3). These
impulses for identification and vicarious pleasure do not,
however, include sexual attraction, and when Philip declares
his love for Maggie, his desire comes in conflict with hers.
At this point, significantly, Philip takes the masculine part,
privileging his desire over Maggie's. Thus, although he
notices 'with a certain pang' that she does not have a sexual
interest in him, he engages in a kind of blackmail when he
tells her that he will be contented to live only if she shows
him that she cares for him. Underlying Philip's bribery is a
basic sense of entitlement regarding the commodity he has
singled out for possession. He says to Maggie, 'If I kept that
little girl in my mind for five years, didn't I earn some part
in her? She ought not to take herself quite away from me'
(5: 1). Here Philip reduces Maggie to an object both by his
financial metaphor and by his address in the third person
(similar to Arthur Donnithorne's condescending use of pronouns in his letter to Hetty). Later, although Maggie does
not appear to recognise that her own desire is absent from

her declaration to Philip, 'I should like always to live with you – to make you happy' (5: 4), he has seen enough of her tendency toward suicidal self-sacrifice to know that these words do not express an active sexual response. Philip is asking Maggie to live according to the same principle of suppression that he has already so eloquently deplored in her.

It is also important to note that Maggie's lack of passion for Philip is not simply or necessarily a result of his physical deformity: an essential element of his love for her is the same sort of 'worship' felt by the vigorous and healthy Gilfil for Tina, and in both cases the adulation of the woman fails to include recognition or accommodation of her desire. Thus Philip is repeatedly perceived by Maggie as looking 'up to her with entreating worship' (6: 10), but his subordinate posture is not one that puts her in a comfortable or happy position. As the narrator satirically comments to his male reader about courtship (in a strategically located paragraph at the beginning of a chapter entitled 'Philip Re-Enters'),

> You . . . presently find yourself in the seat you like best – a little above or a little below the one on which your goddess sits (it is the same thing to the metaphysical mind, and that is the reason why women are at once worshipped and looked down upon). (6: 7)

The problem with Philip's worship is not so much that he openly condescends to Maggie (as Stephen Guest will later), but rather that he regards her as an object, a work of art he desires to possess. He writes in his letter to her,

> perhaps I feel about you as the artist does about the scene over which his soul has brooded with love: he would tremble to see it confided to other hands; he would never believe that it could bear for another all the meaning and the beauty it bears for him. (7: 3)

This is not the first time Philip refers to Maggie as a work of art – he does in fact paint her twice – and his image, which this time reduces Maggie not only to the third person but also to the impersonal pronoun, reveals his tendency to use her as a static and mute object for his own imaginative projections. The narrator's description of him in the novel's Conclusion seems in these terms a comment on Philip's self-serving construction of Maggie, without regard for her desire, as his own private Hamadryad: 'His great companionship was among the trees of the Red Deeps, where the buried joy seemed still to hover – like a revisiting spirit'. For Philip, Maggie's memory serves almost as well as her physical presence, and her desire is equally absent in both.

Maggie's relationship with Stephen Guest both contrasts with and parallels her association with Philip. More obvious are the contrasts: Stephen possesses a physical strength and social charm that Philip lacks, and Maggie's response to him is strongly sexual. From the first scene in which Stephen appears, however, the expectation that he might provide a happy closure either to the plot of personal development or to the romance plot is made seriously questionable. The mock-heroic presentation of his engagement with Lucy Deane – recalling *The Rape of the Lock* in its emphasis on lap dogs, card-playing, scissors and trivial talk – suggests what is borne out by explicit narrative comment: that Stephen's attitudes toward women are condescending and supercilious. Thus he treats courtship as a shallow game, mocking Lucy for her 'feminine tyranny' and asking her to sing 'the whole duty of woman' (6: 1). Underlying Stephen's frivolity, moreover, is the 'tendency to predominance' (6: 7) that in different ways governs his responses to both Lucy and Maggie. He decides to marry Lucy because she is a 'little darling', because there is nothing extreme about her, and because her difference in class gives him scope for a little defiance with his father and sisters (6: 1). He is not very different, in other words, from Maggie's father, who also chose a spouse who would bolster his own sense of power.

Nor is Stephen's attraction to Maggie a turning from triviality to significance. In her case, he is drawn to a challenge represented by the 'delicious opposites' he perceives in her eyes: 'defying and deprecating, contradicting and clinging, imperious and beseeching'. What Stephen desires from Maggie, moreover, is not the free play of these two sides of her personality, but rather the suppression of her defiant side. As the narrator comments, giving expression to Stephen's thought in free indirect discourse, 'To see such a creature subdued by love for one would be a lot worth having' (6: 6). Not surprisingly, the scenes on the boat in which Maggie and Stephen discuss the possibility of elopement are presented as a power struggle that Maggie almost loses when confronted by the same argument Philip had successfully used with her: when Stephen accuses Maggie of making him suffer, she is 'paralysed' by guilt (6: 13). In his possessiveness and in his ability to manipulate Maggie's conscience, Stephen seems merely a cruder version of Philip Wakem.

From the time that *The Mill on the Floss* was first published, readers have complained about Eliot's portrayal of Stephen, but while it may be true that he is unworthy of Maggie, such a judgement presumes as a requirement for the closure of a romance plot the happy conjunction of equally virtuous husband and wife. Eliot's novel, however, stubbornly evades the romance plot that Lucy (who wants Maggie to marry Philip) and Dr Kenn (who thinks she will do best by marrying Stephen), along with many readers, have tried to impose on it: both Philip and Stephen are exposed as imperfect suitors, and the novel's focus is thus shifted away from idealistic notions about courtship to the very question of how desire is constructed. It is significant, therefore, that the narrator should continually emphasise the displaced nature of Maggie's attraction to Stephen. Repeatedly, readers are told that Maggie's susceptibility to him is a symptom of the general deprivation she has been suffering during the six years since her father's bankruptcy. She finds the leisurely life in the Deane household 'intoxicating' (6: 6), and Stephen's adulation appears to her 'hungry nature' as 'the half-remote presence of a world of love and beauty and delight, made up of vague, mingled images from all the poetry and romance she had ever read, or had ever woven in her dreamy reveries' (6: 3). Stephen represents, in other words, all those unattainable ideas of happiness that patriarchal culture has constructed as the objects of feminine desire.

When Maggie rejects Stephen in the name of duty to the past, she is not, therefore, denying her own desire but rather choosing an earlier displacement over a later one: turning away from Stephen, she returns to the world of her brother Tom, who from the beginning has represented her earliest memory of affection and who thus is linked with what she cannot recall – the dyadic union with the mother that precedes entry into the symbolic order. As she tells Philip, 'the first thing I ever remember in my life is standing with Tom by the side of the Floss, while he held my hand: everything before that is dark to me' (5: 1). It is this memory, presumably – not those of the years of strife witnessed by the reader in the first books of the novel – that impels Maggie to reject the romance plot written for her by patriarchy and to return to the script for an equally unattainable aim, that of seeking once again in her relationship with Tom the pre-Oedipal union with the mother, represented here by the darkness that precedes memory.[1] This reversion, paralleled by the generic shift in the novel's plot from *Bildungsroman* and courtship novel to a narrative structure with no distinct conventional antecedents, thus exposes the primordial source of the displaced desires that these more familiar plots express: desire in the symbolic order seeks substitutes for the lost union with the maternal body.

If one looks at the ending of the novel in these terms, then it becomes significant that the mill of its title, which is eventually shattered into pieces by the flood, is often associated with the memory of the past and of the mother. Mr Tulliver, for example, who is most obsessed about the place, links it with his own fragmented memories of his dead mother:

'I remember, the day they finished the malt-house, I thought summat great was to come of it; for we'd a plum-pudding that day and a bit of a feast, and I said to my mother – she was a fine dark-eyed woman, my mother was – the little wench 'ull be like her as two peas.' – Here Mr. Tulliver put his stick between his legs, and took out his snuff-box, for the greater enjoyment of his anecdote, *which dropped from him in fragments, as if he every other moment lost narration in vision* [italics added]. 'I was a little chap no higher much than my mother's knee – she was sore fond of us children, Gritty and me – and so I said to her, "Mother," I said, "shall we have plum-pudding *every* day because o' the malt-house?" She used to tell me o' that till her dying day. She was but a young woman when she died, my mother was.' (3: 9)

Here Tulliver's storytelling style, in which the 'fragments' of 'vision' continually interfere with 'narration', offers a paradigm for the ending of the novel, where the linear 'narration' of the conventional plots gives way to a fragmented and visionary closure that restores Maggie – as she returns to the mill seeking both Tom *and her mother* – to the pre-Oedipal state before sexual difference. The narrator observes, 'brother and sister had gone down in an embrace never to be parted: living through again in one supreme moment the days when they had clasped their little hands in love, and roamed the daisied fields together' (7: 5). At this point, Maggie is seen as returning to the unremembered darkness that preceded the first moment she held hands with Tom while looking at the maternal river. Her heroic rescue of her brother – in which she briefly assumes toward him a masculine role and he appears finally to see her 'with a certain awe and humiliation' (7: 5) – is her last attempt to satisfy her displaced desire for the maternal body, a yearning which Tom has always failed to recognise in his sister.

This final recognition between Maggie and Tom just before they have returned in death to a pre-Oedipal state is not necessarily, however, the apotheosis many have seen it to be. As N. Katherine Hayles has noted, there is a 'division' in the novel between the 'female ethic' espoused by the narrator and the 'givens' of the plot that 'resist' that ethic; moreover, the 'narrator's surmise that Tom is converted remains unsupported' because he remains silent during the rescue, except to utter the name 'Magsie' – hardly proof (and perhaps proof to the contrary) that he has seen the full implications of his sister's rescue.[2] The image of their death as a 'supreme moment' of 'love' in the 'daisied fields' of the past originates, it should be remembered, not in Maggie – who can no longer speak of her experience – but in the narrator, whose own desire for 'early memory' (2: 1) was so clearly established in the opening chapter of dream and reminiscence. If there is an apotheosis at the end of *The Mill on the Floss*, it may be an expression only of the narrator's desire for fulfilment – one which ultimately collides, like Maggie and Tom, with the fragmented machinery of the novel's plot. That the union of the sister and brother can be achieved only in death is itself problematic, after all, and the relationship of this event to the novel's own paradigmatic stories is also discordant and troubling.

Take for example, the legend of St Ogg's, of which the narrator owns 'several manuscript versions' and which is a possible source for the imagery of elevation and sainthood used to describe Maggie's rescue (Tom guesses that Maggie's arrival has been accomplished by an 'almost miraculous divinely-protected effort' [7: 5]). Quoting 'my private hagiographer', the narrator reports that the Virgin, appearing as a woman 'clad in rags' who 'craved to be rowed across the river', was told by the 'men thereabout': ' "Wherefore dost thou desire to cross the river? Tarry till the morning, and take shelter here for the night: so shalt thou be wise, and not foolish." ' Significantly, in refusing the Virgin's 'craving,' these men invoke the same New Testament text about the wise and foolish virgins that Gilfil had used in his sermon attempting to reconcile Tina to her deprivation. St Ogg, in contrast, is the only man to recognise and respond to woman's desire. 'I will ferry thee across: it is enough that thy heart needs it,' he declares; and in response the Virgin offers him her protection: ' "Ogg the son of Beorl, thou art blessed in that thou didst not question and wrangle with the heart's need, but wast smitten with pity, and didst straightway relieve the same" ' (1: 12). Because of her heroic rescue of Tom, Maggie has often been associated with the Virgin of the legend, but if one compares Maggie's story with that of the Virgin, the differences are more striking than the similarities. Unlike the Virgin or St Ogg, Maggie can neither offer protection nor receive it, and her 'heart's need' never goes unquestioned. In her dream while she is on the boat with Stephen, Maggie translates the legend of St Ogg into a parable reflecting her own impossible position, where satisfaction of desire can come only in regression to an imagined childhood: here the Virgin is Lucy, St Ogg is first Stephen and then Tom, and the only state of happiness permitted Maggie emerges from the absence of Tom's anger.

If Maggie's story resembles any narrative inscribed in the text, it is the one she reads in *The History of the Devil* about the woman who is proven to be a witch if she swims and to be innocent if she drowns. Maggie's narrative follows a similar pattern, for her desire – like that of the accused woman and unlike the Virgin's – is denied in either possible case: alive, she will always be guilty in the eyes of patriarchal

St Ogg's; dead, she establishes her innocence and so receives their acclamation in the inscription on the tombstone
she shares with her brother, 'In their death they were not
divided'. This epitaph – also the novel's epigraph – has
often been construed as evidence of the narrative's happy
consummation, but it needs to be remembered that the
words represent the pronouncement, not of Maggie herself
or even of Eliot's narrator, but of unnamed surviving
members of the community of St Ogg's who chose the
inscription. The biblical allusion calls up, moreover, still
another story that excludes woman's desire.[3] The words
from the second Book of Samuel are spoken by David about
the deaths of King Saul and his son Jonathan, who had in
their lives been radically divided by their own conflicting
patriarchal interests: in his jealousy of David's military
accomplishments, Saul had tried repeatedly to kill him –
only to be prevented by the plotting of Jonathan, who loved
David 'as his own soul' (1 Sam. 18: 3). David's lament,
therefore, celebrates the union after conflict not of brother
and sister or of man and woman, but of father and son. It is
followed, moreover, by another impassioned cry by David
for his own beloved Jonathan, a declaration of love between
men: 'thy love to me was wonderful, passing the love of
women' (2 Sam. 1: 26). Maggie and Tom's tombstone is
thus a palimpsest with a grim text underneath its surface:
the story inscribed behind the carved epitaph narrates once
again the exclusion of women from patriarchal ties. The
story of *The Mill on the Floss* represents not the apotheosis
of female desire, but its continuing denial.

Such a reading of the novel's ending, which runs counter
to the narrator's explicit pronouncements about it, is indirectly supported by the plot and style of 'The Lifted Veil',
a story Eliot wrote after stopping the composition of the
early scenes in *The Mill on the Floss*. Interrupting the
progress of the novel at approximately the point when
Eliot's identity was being revealed, this narrative acts as a

subtext that calls into question the authority of her male narrator. Written in the first-person voice of a man who claims powers of prevision, the story exposes both his 'one-sided knowing' and the limitations of realistic writing.[4] Here 'recollections of the past' are revealed as bearing 'hardly a more distinct resemblance to the external reality than the forms of an oriental alphabet to the objects that suggested them' (2) and interpretations of the past, present, or future are seen as subjective projections by the narrator. In this sense, Latimer is an exaggerated version of Eliot's male narrators in *Scenes*, *Adam Bede* and *Mill* – all of whom to a degree render their plots in terms of masculine desire and whose attempts are inevitably futile because the narratives themselves continually undermine the premises of their interpreters. In these terms, 'The Lifted Veil' – Eliot's only first-person narrative – plays an important role in her canon: just as Latimer's story deconstructs his own image of himself and exposes his manipulations of experience, so 'The Lifted Veil' itself calls into question the authority of Eliot's other narrators, whose projections of their desires on to their texts are undermined by the narratives themselves.

After completing 'The Lifted Veil' and *The Mill on the Floss*, Eliot wrote still another short story that stands in uncomfortable opposition to the ostensible meaning of the novel that follows it. Coming immediately before *Silas Marner*, which traces the redemption of the miserly Marner as his lost guineas are transformed into the golden hair of his adopted child Eppie, 'Brother Jacob' traces the nemesis of the grasping and deceiving David Faux, who steals his mother's guineas in order to make his fortune in the West Indies and whose various dishonest schemes are uncovered by his mentally handicapped brother, Jacob. The story also looks backward to *The Mill on the Floss*: while the invocation of the Old Testament David's homoerotic lament suggests Maggie's exclusion from the patriarchal ties that it celebrates, the allusion to the same text in 'Brother Jacob' revises the biblical story itself by dramatising the destructive effect of masculine competition on all forms of love. Here David Faux is like his biblical counterpart in being resourceful and the youngest of many sons. The story of the great king who was loved by Jonathan is disrupted, however, by that of the Old Testament Jacob, whose relationship with his brother Esau was one of competitive struggle: the favourite of his mother, he secured patriarchal authority by bribing Esau and deceiving his father. Eliot's Jacob, also his mother's favourite, unwittingly outwits his brother and then permits his other brother Jonathan to confirm David's duplicity for the world at large. The closure of 'Brother Jacob' thus provides an ironic commentary on the two biblical stories: Eliot's Jacob will certainly never be, like his namesake, the father of twelve tribes; and at Jonathan's death, we can be sure, David will sing no impassioned lament. Nor will David become the king of his people and antitype of a messiah. By its defeat of the aspiring David, Eliot's 'Brother Jacob' undoes its precursor texts, exposing the competitive and hierarchical basis of patriarchal succession.

A similar point can be made about the treatment of the David–Jonathan relationship in Eliot's next work of fiction, *Silas Marner*, which operates ostensibly as a moral fable, but which also stands in questioning dialogue with several of Eliot's earlier fictions.[5] Here the close male bond between Marner and William Dane, which had led the people of Lantern Yard to call them David and Jonathan, is torn asunder by Dane's jealousy and treachery. Described as 'self-complacent' – a word twice used by Latimer in referring to his masculine older brother – Dane (whose name sounds like 'David and Jonathan' conflated into one syllable) wrests from his younger friend both his position of communal authority and his intended wife, leaving Marner, unlike David or Jonathan, bereft of all patriarchal ties. In another sense, however, Marner's fate echoes that of

Jonathan, who was condemned to death by the drawing of lots, but who was saved by the people he, by killing Philistines, had protected. So too Marner is deemed guilty by a drawing of lots in Lantern Yard but is eventually given a patriarchal position in the community of Raveloe – not, however, in gratitude for his military exploits, but rather for his maternal nurturing of the orphaned Eppie. The story's fable, therefore – as overdetermined in its closure as 'Brother Jacob', with its 'fine peripateia' (2) – both interrogates and restores patriarchal values: on the one hand, it is the feminine qualities in Marner that save him, but, on the other hand, he is rewarded by receiving a masculine position in the community – while the masculine qualities in the female characters remain, for the most part, as repressed as they are in the conclusion of *The Mill on the Floss*.

The continual emphasis in *Silas Marner* on chance makes the comparison with *Mill* especially relevant. Silas is victimised by chance at the drawing of lots but is also rewarded by it when Eppie toddles into his cottage: as a man, in other words, he is subject to the vagaries of fortune, but has the potential to win fate's wager. Maggie's fate, however, is determined not by the drawing of lots – which would give her a 50 per cent chance of winning – but by the witch-test, which provides the chance only for two different kinds of loss: the various 'lots' determined by chance in the world of men are reduced in female experience to death or the narrow 'lot' belonging even to the ideal wife Nancy Lammeter (17). Silas's fulfilment at the conclusion of his moral fable represents, therefore, exactly the happiness that is unachievable in Maggie Tulliver's female *Bildungsroman*. In *Silas Marner*, moreover, as in Eliot's other works, the denial or subduing of woman's desire functions as a destabilising force in the narrative, exposing in the story's very fulfilment the female losses that have led to the achievement of such a closure.

Beginning even with Marner, one finds feminine loss

underlying the plot's presentation of masculine fulfilment –
though Silas himself is not the agent of that loss. As
numerous critics have noted, Marner's maternal response to
Eppie can be traced back directly to his dead mother and
sister, from whom he takes the child's name (no mention is
ever made of his father). Silas's herb cures, displaced first
by his religious guilt and then by his miserliness, were
learned from his mother. These temporarily give him a
status in Raveloe, comparable to that of the 'Wise Woman
at Tarley', until he is seen as a threat to the authority of Dr
Kimble, whose reputation is based solely on his patriarchal
succession: 'Time out of mind the Raveloe doctor had been
a Kimble' (11). Then, after Marner has found Eppie, her
clean clothes (washed by Dolly Winthrop) seem like 'fresh-
sprung herbs', and his play with her in the fields returns
him to the 'familiar' healing plants of his distant past. So too
Marner's cherished brown earthenware pot, shattered into
fragments when he goes during his miserly phase in quest of
the maternal element of 'fresh clear water' (2), is finally
associated by the narrator with the feminine hearth of the
home he makes for Eppie: 'he loved the old brick hearth as
he had loved his brown pot – and was it not there when he
had found Eppie?' (16). The discovery of Eppie is thus for
Silas a return to the maternal love he had received from his
mother and transferred to his younger sister, 'whom he had
carried about in his arms for a year before she died' (12).

The maternal does not bring the same unmixed happiness
to the female characters that it does to Silas, however. Even
Dolly Winthrop, the most idealised woman in the story next
to Eppie, must live with a man who drinks, and she unquestioningly submits to this predicament as if it were
determined by nature. She accepts her husband's habit, we
are told, 'considering that "men *would* be so", and viewing
the stronger sex in the light of animals whom it had pleased
Heaven to make naturally troublesome, like bulls and
turkey-cocks' (10). Dolly's only complaint about Ben

Winthrop is made indirectly, as she remarks on Marner's potential for child-rearing: 'I've seen men as are wonderful handy wi' children. The men are awk'ard and contrairy mostly, God help 'em – but when the drink's out of 'em, they aren't unsensible, though they're bad for leeching and bandaging – so fiery and unpatient' (14). Interestingly, it is precisely when she is 'leeching or poulticing' that Dolly herself finds her thoughts becoming 'opportunities of illumination' (16) for sorting out the problems of others, including Marner. Winthrop is thus seen as lacking exactly the patience that gives Dolly her unlettered instinctive knowledge. Another indirect recognition of Winthrop's tendency to unpleasantness and insensitivity emerges in Marner's comment, a veiled allusion to the selfish father, about Aaron's kindnesses: 'He's his mother's lad' (16). Significantly, the reader is made much more aware of the relationship between Dolly and Marner as joint 'parents' of Eppie than of that between Dolly and her husband as parents of Aaron and three other sons. Dolly and Ben are never seen together, in fact, until the Conclusion, and when we are told that Dolly walked behind the bride and groom 'with her husband', the very symmetry of the scene points to the discordance that Ben represents in Dolly's life.

Another discordance in the Conclusion that leads back into a conflict within the story can be seen in the decision by Godfrey Cass to leave his wife Nancy home alone on the day of Eppie's marriage. Nancy Lammeter is presented from the beginning as a feminine ideal. Beautiful, submissive and thrifty, she is seen by everyone in Raveloe as the most valuable commodity on the village marriage market, potentially a dutiful wife and 'a saving to the old Squire, if she never brought a penny to her fortune' (3). In Nancy's perfect adherence to the ideal, however, she reveals that the 'propriety and moderation' of the standard angel of the hearth (11) imply as well a deadening rigidity caused by a commitment to hollow romantic notions. It is folly, for example, for her to decide that

> not the most dazzling rank should induce her to marry a man whose conduct showed him careless of his character, but that 'love once, love always', was the motto of a true and pure woman, and no man should ever have any right over her which would be a call on her to destroy the dried flowers that she treasured, and always would treasure for Godfrey Cass's sake. (11)

After her marriage to Cass, this self-destructive thinking takes the form of an irrational refusal to adopt a child – the very action that in Silas's plot (and Janet Dempster's plot before it) brings happiness and renewal. Typically, Nancy fears that adoption would constitute defiance of a patriarchal deity, an attempt 'wilfully and rebelliously' to '*choose your lot* in spite of Providence' [italics added]. The result is that part of Nancy's 'lot' – unrelated to chance – is having to tolerate her husband's 'rough answers and unfeeling words' in response to their childlessness (17), a mode of behaviour that she takes to be as natural as Dolly deems Ben's drinking to be. Nancy had already seen such behaviour, after all, in her father, whom she trusted completely even though he was 'a little hot and hasty now and then' (11). Nancy's absolute dependence on the idea of masculine authority makes her, in short, its perennial victim, and Silas Marner's adoption of Godfrey's child simultaneously calls into question the myth of patriarchal succession that has formed her thinking.

Ironically, if there is any woman in the novel who escapes Nancy's assumptions about masculine authority, it is her 'cheerful-looking' older sister Priscilla, who, like Marner, deftly crosses gender lines in her assumption of roles generally attributed to the other sex. Priscilla, in fact, is subtly linked to Marner and his transformation by matern-

ity, for it is her 'present' of pork that is hanging over
Marner's hearth on the night he is robbed. Her kindness to
Marner precedes, in other words, that of the women who
offer him sympathy only after he has adopted Eppie. This
gesture, moreover, cannot be construed simply as evidence
of Priscilla's deference to men. Although she is an 'excellent
housewife' (5) and submits to Nancy's absurd insistence
that they dress alike, she likes 'to see the men mastered!'
and laughs at her own failure to meet masculine standards of
beauty: 'The pretty uns do for fly-catchers – they keep the
men off us' (11). Like the victimised and isolated spinsters
of Eliot's earlier fictions, Priscilla assumes the daughterly
office of caring for her elderly father, but, unlike them, she
then uses that position literally to '[take] the reins' out of his
hands and to assume an active role in 'outdoor management'
– thus establishing for herself a 'lot' much wider than
Nancy's, which is confined to her husband's 'house and
garden'. Priscilla becomes 'manager', in fact, of both her
father and his farm. Cleverly, she justifies her appropriation
of masculine power by presenting it as a means of protecting
her father's health and authority:

'And reason good as I should manage you, father,' said
Priscilla, 'else you'd be giving yourself your death with
rheumatism. And as for the farm, if anything turns out
wrong, as it can't but do in these times, there's nothing
kills a man so soon as having nobody to find fault with but
himself. It's a deal the best way o' being master, to let
somebody else do the ordering, and keep the blaming in
your own hands. It 'ud save many a man a stroke, *I*
believe.' (17)

These manipulations of her father's sense of masculine
mastery allow Priscilla to defy chance and to take her fate
into her own hands. As she says of her pork-pies, 'they
don't turn out well by chance' (11). It is also Priscilla who

urges Nancy to leave the domestic hearth for a managerial job of her own: 'My dear, . . . you'll never be low when you've got a dairy' (17).

Even Priscilla must admit, however, that she can remain single and independent only because of her privileged position in the class structure. More valuable to her than the physical attributes that would make her, like her sister, desirable in the marriage market is a father whose business can provide her with an arena for active engagement in the world of business: 'but, thank God! my father's a sober man and likely to live; and if you've got a man by the chimney-corner, it doesn't matter if he's childish – the business needn't be broke up'. Priscilla knows that she is luckier than some women, who are driven to marriage because they 'have got no fortin, and can't help themselves' (11). Her position, moreover, is not altogether secure: the unspoken agenda in her repeated references to her father's potential longevity is that her own income and access to the world of men is dependent on his survival. Even Priscilla, who is better able than the other women in the novel to manipulate the power structures of patriarchy, requires a masculine sponsor in order to conduct her life outside the 'house and garden' – another version of Milly Barton's 'four walls' – to which the married woman is confined.

If the contrast between the Lammeter sisters offers two alternative female fates, the 'lot' of Molly Farren Cass presents a third – and a horrific – feminine role. In spite of her marriage, which because of its concealment offers her no protection or status, Molly's fate is remarkably similar to that of Hetty Sorrel. Like Hetty, she is drawn to her secret lover by the trappings of his class. Like Hetty, too, she invites complex and contradictory responses from Eliot's narrator, and her story stands out from that of other characters for its radical incompleteness. The two narratives of Hetty and Molly can be seen, in fact, as matching fragments, each supplementing the other: just as Hetty's seduction by Arthur is presented in detail while the particulars of her death are strikingly evaded, so Molly's death is closely delineated while her marriage to Godfrey Cass is only vaguely referred to as the burdensome consequence *for him* of a moment of 'low passion' (3). Both heroines, moreover, like Lucy of 'Janet's Repentance', indirectly create male happiness by dying. Only after Molly's actual death can Silas Marner really be 'a dead man come to life again' (1).

The narrative is not explicitly constructed, however, to elicit sympathy for Molly in her effective martyrdom. One of the limitations placed on her depiction is the narrator's habit, especially at the outset, of referring to Molly only in free indirect discourse that expresses Godfrey's attitude toward her. It is thus chiefly by oblique means that the narrative draws attention to the victimisation of 'the unhappy woman' (3) who eventually seeks 'vengeance' (12) on the man who desired her body but came to loathe her person. The single allusion to Molly's own point of view, for example – that she was attracted to Godfrey as the focus for an imagined 'barmaid's paradise of pink ribbons and gentleman's jokes' (12) – points indirectly to her vulnerability (again, like Hetty's) because of her subordinate position in the class system. Molly's pathetic Edenic fantasy is basically no different from that of Godfrey himself, moreover, who sees the orderly Lammeter household as a 'paradise' (3) with potential for transforming his life.

An even more indirect allusion to Molly's position occurs in the first chapter that mentions her, which ends with a seemingly insignificant incident where Godfrey – driven to distraction by Dunstan's threat to disclose his shameful past – leaves for the Rainbow to 'hear the talk about the cockfighting'. At that point, we are told,

Snuff, the brown spaniel, who had placed herself in front of him, and had been watching him for some time, now

jumped up in impatience for the expected caress. But
Godfrey thrust her away without looking at her, and left
the room, followed humbly by the unresenting Snuff –
perhaps because she saw no other career open to her.
(3)

In this small paradigm for sexual relationships in the novel,
the male rudely refuses to the female the physical affection
that is her only possible 'career'. Godfrey's demeanour
toward his pointedly female spaniel thus recalls his rejection
of Molly, anticipates his brusqueness to Nancy, and alludes
to the powerlessness of both his wives to find another
'career'. Molly, like the other women in the novel, is
confined to the role assigned her by patriarchy, and her
decision to reveal her marriage to Cass constitutes an
assertion of the only rights she has.

For this reason, the chapter describing Molly's walk
through the snow toward the Red House – a parallel with
and contrast to Hetty's journey in quest of Arthur – can
evoke a whole range of contradictory responses. Sand-
wiched in between accounts of the dance at which Godfrey
is seen with the woman he now desires, the depiction of
Molly's movements serves as an interruption of and interference with Godfrey's romance plot. Sympathy for Molly is
diminished especially by her addiction to 'the demon Opium'
– a detail which, as the response to Janet Dempster's
drinking had already revealed, would have invited the
opprobrium of many Victorian readers. The veiled allusion
to Janet could also serve to vindicate Molly, however, by
reminding the reader of the possible causes of the woman's
addiction. Though not abused like Janet, Molly has been
deserted by her husband and has been left with no other
'career' except that of being 'enslaved, body and soul', to
the drug that will allow her to forget what happened to her –
a literal version, in fact, of Godfrey's own strategy, described
in the opening sentence of the chapter about Molly's death,

of 'taking draughts of forgetfulness from the sweet presence of Nancy' (12). Molly's addiction to opium makes her less 'forgetful', moreover, than Godfrey's analogous use of Nancy: while Molly gives up to the drug all consciousness except that of her child – whom she holds in an 'instinctive clutch' until the moment she dies – Godfrey puts both his wife and his child out of his mind in an attempt to forget his past and eventually even hopes for Molly's death. In this respect, he is more like Hetty than Molly is.[6] Godfrey and Hetty are similarly self-protective in denying the existence of their progeny, while Molly guards the child even as she destroys herself.

The powerful but problematic presence of Molly Cass in *Silas Marner* disrupts even the novel's ostensibly satisfying closure, in which Eppie rejects her biological father while favouring the adoptive parent and completes the family circle by marrying a man who will play the role of son to Silas Marner (forebodingly anticipating Romola's destructive marriage). All of the characters who have borne a significant relationship to Eppie are somehow present at her marriage: Marner plays the parental role he deserves and Dolly occupies the double place of godmother and mother of the groom, while Nancy and Godfrey Cass – though absent – supply the wedding dress and party. Only Molly's implied presence in the novel's closure is ignored by the narrator, who in ending the story describes the garden at Stone-pits, where 'the flowers shone with answering gladness, as the four united people came within sight of them'. What is left unmentioned here, significantly, is that the garden which stands as an image of this new union contains the furze-bush (conventionally associated with the fallen woman) on which Molly's corpse was found, which Eppie had transplanted in her mother's memory. Molly Cass's death – the event which had made possible the happiness of the wedding party – is thus subliminally present in the novel's ending and, in spite of the narrator's failure to mention it, stands as a reminder of the loss that has accomplished the happy closure.

Nor is the seeming symmetry of the 'four united people' without its nagging loose ends. Marner and Dolly, for example, can appear as a couple here only because Winthrop has just 'found it agreeable to turn in' at the Rainbow rather than going back to the house with his family (Conclusion). Nor is the marriage of Aaron and Eppie necessarily an image of perfect harmony. Though the relationship is generally presented in the idealised terms of fairy tale, the narrator has offered one hint of Eppie's frustrated desire for knowledge and power. When Marner proposes the visit to Lantern Yard, Eppie is

> very joyful, for there was the prospect not only of wonder and delight at seeing a strange country, but also of coming back to tell Aaron all about it. Aaron was so much wiser than she was about most things – it would be rather pleasant to have this little advantage over him. (21)

Even in the overdetermined happy closure of Eliot's most fable-like novel are veiled references to a suppression of women that is necessary for the construction of happy patriarchal families. By definition, the romance plot requires that the fulfilment of Marner and Aaron be more complete than that of Dolly and Eppie. Behind this asymmetrical closure, moreover, stands the plot whose own closure has enabled the resolution of the romance plot. Like Lucy and Hetty, Molly – Eliot's only married fallen woman and another lost mother – must die before the patriarchal family can achieve its happy consummation.

5 *Romola* to *The Spanish Gypsy*: Fictions of Gender and History

Eliot's next novel, *Romola*, represents a radical departure from *Silas Marner*, in terms both of setting and of plot: here Eliot moves the action of her narrative to fifteenth-century Italy, and it closes with a description of what appears to be the first matriarchal family in Eliot's fiction. From the beginning, *Romola* has been the subject of hostile criticism directed at both its preponderance of historical detail and its failure to focus exclusively on Savonarola, its historical hero. In recent years, however, some critics have responded to such objections by equating Romola Bardi's experience with 'man's moral history' and tracing in the novel's plot the narrative patterns of the epic, the morality play, the allegory, the fable, the *Bildungsroman*, and, most recently, the '"continuous historical" apocalypse'.[1] Most of these readings concentrate on the stages of Romola's personal development: from her early attachment to a pagan father, through her phase of commitment to Savonarola's Christianity, and finally to her independent assumption of a new sympathetic morality – viewed by many as analogous to Comte's Religion of Humanity. Such a teleological reading is complicated, however, not only by its unquestioning assumption of a myth of historical progression, but also by the fact that Eliot has chosen as her emblematic human figure a female character whose place in her historical setting is overdetermined by her gender. Although Eliot in her depiction of Romola's unhappy marriage writes beyond the conventional ending of the romance plot, her closure of the quest plot is made problematic by the limitations placed on her heroine by her culture's construction of gender. There is a pervasive tension in the novel, therefore, between the teleological thrust of its historical plot and the static repetitiveness of its gender plot, which consistently places its heroine in positions of subordination to men.

The gender plot in *Romola* is apparent even in the novel's Proem, in which the Spirit of a fifteenth-century man speaks nostalgically of the Florentine streets 'where he inherited the eager life of his fathers' and ponders the fate of his city with questions that reflect a view of history based entirely on masculine struggles for power:

> How has it all turned out? Which party is likely to be banished and have its houses sacked just now? Is there any successor of the incomparable Lorenzo ... ? And what famous scholar is dictating the Latin letters of the Republic – what fiery philosopher is lecturing on Dante in the Duomo ... ?

The only references to women made by the Spirit of the Age presume their subordinate status as nursemaids, daughters, or – in the case of the Madonna Annunziata – idealised emblems of chaste submission. The narrator, however – like the speaker in *Adam Bede* who challenges Townley's perspective – rejects the Spirit's preoccupation with masculine hegemony and directs his eye to the abiding human presence in Florence, its 'upturned living faces, and lips moving to the old prayers for help'. These two conflicting attitudes to history – one based on struggles for power, the other on what Eliot repeatedly called 'sympathy' – remain in opposition throughout the novel: the narrative that follows the Proem answers the Spirit's questions, but in so doing exposes the narrowness and destructiveness of his curiosity about the vagaries of political and intellectual sovereignty.

This strategy of interrogating the very questions it

answers is not immediately apparent in *Romola*, however, for the novel's most explicitly historical scenes arouse intense curiosity about the struggles for supremacy that took place when Florence was 'orphaned' (4) by the loss of its presiding patriarch, Lorenzo de' Medici. The early chapters are, in fact, confusing to the reader looking for an explanation of the novel's title. The first mention of Romola does not come until the end of the third chapter – Nello alludes to her as worth seeing along with Bardo's scholarly 'collections' – and the reader does not encounter her directly until Chapter 5, in which she is seen as a static emblem of daughterly devotion. The first four chapters of the novel establish a context for this scene, however, by depicting the masculine world that requires the subordination of Romola and other women to the men who father and marry them.

In the early chapters of *Romola*, for example, the reader watches Tito Melema embraced by a closely knit male culture, imaged especially in 'Apollo and the Razor', the barber-shop described by its owner Nello as 'the focus of Florentine intellect'. Here Tito's 'initiation into the mysteries of the razor' is presented as a male rite of passage leading to inspiration. In an inversion of the Samson story that excludes Delilah altogether, Machiavelli links 'delicate shaving' with sharpness of intellect (3), while Nello promises Tito that his new appearance will bring him power and women. The market-place that sustains Nello's barber-shop is a world in which women are casually associated with other objects of exchange. Bratti, explaining his absence from his shop, declares, 'I've got a wife and a raven to stay at home and mind the stock'. The same equation of women with animals appears in Nello's comments about the ominous signs following upon Lorenzo's death: 'several cows and women have had still-born calves this Quaresima; and for the bad eggs that have been broken since the Carnival, nobody has counted them' (1).

Nello's failure to distinguish between cows and women is echoed in the presentation of Tessa, the only sharply defined female character in the novel's opening chapters. Bratti first offers to take Tito to Tessa, 'the prettiest damsel in the Mercato' (1), if Tito will give him in exchange information about himself. Tito refuses this masculine bargain and decides instead to spend a 'medium of exchange' that cannot be used against him by other men: since he has no money, he sets out to confer his affection on any damsel who will feed him and thus to 'get [his] breakfast for love' (2). Tito's strategy of earning his milk by kissing Tessa is interestingly close to female prostitution, but its results could not be more different: in this masculine economy, Tito can spend his sexuality freely and widely without loss because as a man he is an agent rather than an object of exchange. Tessa, however, is from the first moment she appears a commodity to be bought and sold. Tito glimpses her, not only with the milk that she sells, but also with the mules that bear it to market, whose 'red tassels and collars' are visually repeated in Tessa's own 'red hood' (2); she appears as a particularised version of 'the hardy, scant-feeding peasant-women' who stream into the city 'with a year's labour in a moderate bundle of yarn on their backs' (14) – yarn that eventually finds its way into the sack of the swindling Bratti. In the sexual economy of *Romola*, female bodies and female labour are continually consumed by the market's masculine traders.

When Romola is finally introduced in Chapter 5, she too is seen as a performer of work useful to men – though because of her class she does not bear the fruits of her labour on her back. Romola reads to her father Bardo, but is assumed by him not to have the intelligence to interpret what she reads. Bardo's basic misogyny is apparent in his cursing references to lamiae and harpies, as well as in his praise of Romola for being different from 'the herd of [her] sex' and having 'a man's nobility of soul'. Like Maggie

Tulliver, Romola is considered inferior to her brother, unqualified to use her mind because it is enclosed in a female body. Romola's only way of pleasing her father, therefore, is to bring him a replacement for the son who had abandoned him. The novel's courtship scenes, in which Bardo's erotic attraction to Tito is carefully depicted, seem an ideal fulfilment of Romola's resolve to find a substitute son for her father. Long before the first kiss between Romola and Tito, Bardo has lingeringly touched Tito's hand, hair and face. The focus of the proposal scene is Tito's role, not as a husband, but as a son, and Romola seems absent altogether from the arrangements for her marriage. In their sexual relationship, Tito encourages Romola to be passive, 'subdued into mere enjoyment' (17) like the image of Ariadne in his own altered version of 'The Triumph of Bacchus'. The financial arrangements for the marriage are made not only by Bardo and Tito, but also by Bernardo del Nero, Romola's godfather, who suggests that Tito support Bardo financially 'in place of the *morgen-cap*' (19) – thus handing over to Romola's father the money paid to a bride on the morning after her wedding. It is not surprising, therefore, that it is Bernardo who tells Bardo with regard to Romola, 'thou hast a rare gem of thy own; take care no one gets it who is not likely to pay a worthy price' (6). Though Bernardo's tone is certainly less coarse than Nello's when he describes Romola as Bardo's 'virgin gold' (8), the underlying assumptions of the two men are the same: Romola is for both an object of exchange.

That such different characters as Nello and Bernardo should have similar views about women is a comment less on them than on the patriarchal culture in which they live, which is described with great particularity in precisely those scenes of Florentine life that many critics have declared to be extraneous. Eliot's famous defence of the historical material in *Romola*, that 'It is the habit of my imagination to strive after as full a vision of the medium in which a character moves as of the character itself' (*GEL* 4: 97), can apply as much to gender as to other culturally determined ideologies. The force of gender definitions is vividly apparent, for example, in the novel's Florentine festivals, all of which are dominated by grotesque images of masculine supremacy. The feast of San Giovanni culminates in the appearance of 'the car of the Zecca or Mint', displaying on its thirty-foot summit 'a living representative of St John the Baptist'. The saintly figure is linked by the narrator not only to Florence's money but also to its pagan patron, Mars: though the statue of 'the Man-destroyer' no longer stands on the banks of the Arno, we are told, 'spear and shield could be hired by gold florins, and on the gold florins there had always been the image of San Giovanni' (8).

The Peasants' Fair, held on the feast of the Nativity of the Virgin, seems a contrast with the masculine and mercenary feast of San Giovanni. Here the reader is presented with a procession not of male Florentine worthies but of 'barefooted, hard-heeled contadine' with 'sun-dried, bronzed faces' and 'strange, fragmentary garb, dim with hereditary dirt'. These women, however – clothed with signs of their closeness to the earth rather than with signs of power – proceed to the Church of the Nunziata, where they find themselves competing with 'another multitude', a 'crowd of votive waxen images, the effigies of great personages' and 'Florentines of high name': 'popes, emperors, kings, cardinals, and famous condottieri'. These images, 'spreading high and far over the walls and ceiling' and 'pressing close against each other, that they might be nearer the potent Virgin' (14), are the permanent presences in the Church, the real embodiments of power in Florence (the Spirit of the Age recalls in the Proem that he also was represented by such a waxen image in the church). Here the 'potent Virgin' is fetishised as a hollow, desexualised, and abstract image of woman, a phallic emblem and a focus for male power. A privileging of masculine hegemony is equally apparent in the street scenes of the Peasants' Fair: Bratti uses 'mercantile coquetry' to swindle superstitious peasant women, and the conjuror advertises sham marriage ceremonies that can be 'dissolved . . . at every man's own will and pleasure' (14).

A masculine pleasure-principle also dominates the celebration of the Carnival, depicted in its pagan guise on the day of Romola's betrothal and in its Christian incarnation after Savonarola has instituted the Pyramid of Vanities. In the first celebration, 'boys and striplings' demand tribute money of everyone in the crowd and conclude the evening with 'the standing entertainment of stone-throwing', which, the narrator comments in free indirect discourse that mimics the thoughts of the boys, 'was not entirely monotonous, since the consequent maiming was various, and it was not always a single person who was killed' (20). In the second carnival, the same boys – now transformed by Savonarola into 'beardless inquisitors' (49) – demand tribute money for their red crosses and humiliate women by stripping them of all decoration. Monna Brigida suffers a horrible indignity at the hands of these 'cherubic' boys (51), and Tessa – who is harrassed or assaulted at all three of the novel's festivals – is rescued from them by Romola only at the last minute.

A more sinister version of the crude masculine aggression of the street festivals takes place, behind closed doors and among the most politically powerful men of the city, at the supper in the Ruccelai Gardens. Like the gatherings in the barber shop, this scene is erotically charged, as alliances of power and influence are formed between men. Attempting to cajole Tito into their conspiracy, Tornabuoni puts his leg across Tito's knee and caresses his ankle, while Pucci lays his hand on Tito's shoulder. At the meal itself, a parody of Christ's last supper, the 'expensive toughness' of the sacramental meal – an unplucked peacock, comically suggestive of male vanity – makes it inedible. Even these men, the narrator tells us, would have preferred 'the vulgar digestibility of capon', but were not 'bold' enough to ask for the softer flesh of the castrated bird (39).

Though most of the male characters in *Romola* participate in these rituals of male bonding, the contrasting behaviour of the artist Piero di Cosimo refutes the notion that such activities are necessarily or essentially male. Though he does not allow Nello to shave off his beard, Piero has, in fact, the sharpest intelligence in the novel. He is the only character to see Romola's position clearly, as like that of Antigone in both her classic situations: loyal daughter of a blind father and defier of patriarchal authority. Piero does not, what's more, play masculine power games – even his misogyny seems parodic mimicry – and, as if to identify himself with the feminine, he lives exclusively on eggs, opening his door only to the young girl who delivers them. Piero's unique position in the plot of *Romola* challenges the ideology of rigid gender definitions. Significantly, it is he who in the novel's Epilogue disapproves of Romola's altar to Savonarola.

While the masculine world of *Romola* is depicted in punctilious detail, the circumstances of its heroine are often hidden in narrative gaps that undermine the illusion of narrative continuity and challenge the teleological movement of the conventional plot. One of the most significant of these occurs between Books One and Two, where the story leaps from the betrothal, set during the carnival of 1492, to the appearance of the French king in Florence, which takes place in November of 1494, more than eighteen months after the marriage of Romola and Tito (which is never depicted). Absent too from the chronological narrative is an account of Bardo's death, which takes place in the late summer of 1494 but is not described until it is reported through Romola's memory three months later. A result of these breaks in narrative continuity is that the focus is shifted from Romola and Tito's sexual consummation to its unhappy aftermath and from the drama of Romola's shock at the loss of her father to its effect on her marriage. This foreshortening moves the narrative forward immediately to the crises in Romola's relationship with Tito, presented as a series of chilling struggles for 'mastery' – most of which he wins because of his power as husband. As he says to Romola in a sentence startlingly free of logical connectives, 'The event is irrevocable, the library is sold, and you are my wife' (32).

Romola's marriage looks backward to Janet Dempster's physical abuse and forward to the disastrous marriages of Dorothea Brooke and Gwendolen Harleth. But perhaps because of the distancing effect created by the Renaissance Italian setting, Eliot is never more daring than in *Romola* in allowing her heroine to abandon an unhappy marriage. The process is depicted in several stages, as Romola gradually frees herself from the belief that she must stay in a 'degrading servitude' (56). Her first flight from Tito is stopped by Savonarola, who quickly reduces her to passivity by addressing her as 'my daughter' (40). Significantly, this assumption by Savonarola of a paternal role deters Romola from seeking out Cassandra Fedele, the greatest female scholar of Italy. Conversion to Savonarola's ideals constitutes a return to patriarchy.

It can be argued that there is a value in Savonarola's insistence on Romola's responsibility to the people of Florence. His emphasis on 'the debt of a wife' (40) is troubling, however, for Romola has just felt relief at escaping 'the breath of soft hated lips warm upon her cheek' (37). Appearing 'as if the words were being wrung from her', she confesses that she has lost her sexual feelings for Tito: 'My husband . . . he is not . . . my love is gone!' When Savonarola responds by speaking of a 'higher love' that is not 'carnal', Romola reverts to the issue he is evading, that if she goes back to Tito he may require a sexual response from her: '"Yet if – oh, how could I bear – "'. Romola, we are told by the narrator, 'had involuntarily begun to say something which she sought to banish from her mind again'. These are Romola's last words of protest, and Savonarola's answer to her inarticulate desperation is to urge self-sacrifice: 'Make your marriage-sorrows an offering too, my daughter' (40). After this scene, there is another significant gap, and Romola is not described until twenty-two months later, when she is seen ministering to the sick in the streets of Florence and so fulfilling Savonarola's injunction that she carry out her responsibilities as a 'daughter of Florence' (41). The absence, however, of any references to the sexual implications of Romola's return to Tito makes this fulfilment incomplete and unsatisfying. The issue of Tito's possession of Romola's sexuality, so dramatically raised in her dialogue with Savonarola, is left unresolved, a wide fissure in the conventional plot that attempts to give meaning to Romola's return to Florence.

Romola's second decision to leave her marriage is made 'without any counsel of her godfather or of Savonarola' (56). In what F.R. Leavis called a scene 'embarrassingly like a girlhood dream',[2] Romola rejects all sources of authority and in a mood of 'new rebellion' and 'new despair' drifts off in a sailboat in quest of death or 'a new life' (61). As far as the gender plot is concerned, this sequence represents Romola's only full break from the masculine hegemony of Florence. A salient detail in such a reading is that Romola gets the idea to drift off to sea from a story in the *Decameron*, the book she had read furtively for her own pleasure while her father was asleep and whose destruction in the Pyramid of Vanities Piero laments. Gostanza's story, grouped in Boccaccio with the tales of lovers 'who won happiness after grief or misfortune',[3] is significantly different, however, from Romola's. Gostanza's despair stems not from dead affection but from the belief that her lover is dead, and her suicidal journey finally brings her to marriage and happiness. Romola's experience is an inversion of Gostanza's, an escape from patriarchy rather than a return to it. Coming not before her marriage but in the wake of its embittering deterioration, Romola's transformation lies in her role – not unlike that of Savonarola in Florence – of moral leadership: the romance plot has given way to the quest plot. Interestingly, Romola's guidance is offered first of all to men: a fifteen-year-old boy and a priest pathetic in his fear of the plague.

Eliot's adaptation of Boccaccio's story is also different from the original because it is embedded in an otherwise realistic and historical narrative. Romola's departure to a place without a name where she becomes the subject not of written history but of oral legend has often been troubling to critics, many of whom see the incident as a form of escapism on Eliot's part – a retreat from her historical subject into an imagined world of romance. In terms of the gender plot, however, this device seems appropriate, for Romola's lack of engagement in political life is as much a historical contingency as Tito's and Savonarola's immersion in it. She is unable to find a place in the history of Florence except as a wife or daughter, and so her 'new life' begins in a place where she is not known to occupy either of these subordinate roles. That this shift in Romola's position requires a radical departure from the plot's heretofore realistic technique is a dramatic manifestation of the restrictions of gender in the novel's 'realistic' world. It is worth noting that this scene, like the flood scene at the end of *The Mill on the Floss*, was part of Eliot's original conception of the novel, not a desperate attempt to escape from the complexities of an unmanageable plot. In both cases, the departure from 'realistic' narrative form is a commentary on the masculine power structure it depicts: the gender plot takes over from the progressive historical plot and moves the action into a realm outside patriarchy. Because the historical novel is traditionally male territory, Eliot's adaptation of the genre must somehow abandon its conventions in order to accommodate the female subject.

This generic shift is apparent in the imagery used to describe Romola's state of mind as she drifts in the boat:

> Memories hung upon her like the weight of broken wings that could never be lifted – memories of human sympathy which even in its pains leaves a thirst that the Great Mother has no milk to still. Romola felt orphaned in those wide spaces of sea and sky. She read no message of love for her in that far-off symbolic writing of the heavens, and with a great sob she wished that she might be gliding into death.
>
> She drew the cowl over her head again and covered her face, choosing darkness rather than the light of the stars, which seemed to her like the hard light of eyes that looked at her without seeing her. (61)

Here the images used to describe Romola's feelings parallel her actual orphaned state: like Latimer of 'The Lifted Veil' – who also associates the mother with darkness and water and the father with penetrating but distorting sight – she had lost her mother as a child and was then deprived of love by a father who immersed himself in 'symbolic writing' and, like the stars, 'looked at her without seeing her'. In a sense, when Romola draws the cowl (a pun on 'caul'?) over her face and covers her eyes, she is effecting a reverse birth, a return to the womb.[4] It is significant, therefore, that when she awakens, she finds herself in a place described in images associated with a maternal body: her flight from Florence and masculine authority allows a return to pre-Oedipal union with the mother.

From this perspective, it is tempting to see the plague-village sequence as a solution to the dilemmas portrayed in the earlier chapters of *Romola* – a genuine 'girlhood dream', though not in the sense that Leavis meant. To see the novel in this way, however, would be to impose on it another teleological reading and to ignore the destabilising elements

both in these scenes and in the Epilogue – elements that
show the gender plot deconstructing the fulfilment even of
the quest plot. Romola's idealisation by the people of the
plague-village can also be seen, for example, as a continua-
tion of her position as object. Tito, after all, had also
idealised her, and the patriarchs of Florence had carried the
Madonna of L'Impruneta – another 'potent Virgin' that is
really a totem of male power – in the name of both
protection and conquest. As Margaret Homans has recently
written, Romola

> is in [the plague-village] scene a holy object of beauty,
> spied upon by profane male eyes, much as Tiresias spied
> upon Minerva in the passage from Politian Romola once
> read to her father. ... To be a mother, even the
> Madonna, ... is also to be the maternal body so feared by
> Western culture.[5]

That Eliot herself saw the dangerous implications of idealisation is apparent in her essay on Margaret Fuller and Mary
Wollstonecraft, published in 1855, in which she translates
the words of the Roman magnates about Romulus: 'let him
be a god, provided he be not living'. Eliot then comments,
'and so men say of women, let them be idols, useless
absorbents of precious things, provided we are not obliged
to admit them to be strictly fellow-beings, to be treated, one
and all, with justice and sober reverence'. Eliot's remarks
are interesting for what they reveal about her views on her
own patriarchal culture, but also for the light they may cast
on the novel's title (*Romola* is the only Eliot novel to bear a
woman's name). The word 'Romola' does not exist in Italian
except as a name for a hill outside Florence. Eliot adapted
the word for her own purposes and told a correspondent
that she had based it on 'Romola', the 'Italian equivalent of
Romulus' (*GEL* 4: 174). In the light of these facts, Romola's
name might be linked not only to her epic role, as some

critics have suggested, but also to her idealised position in
the eyes of men. It is worth noting that just before intro-
ducing her translation of the passage about Romulus, Eliot
complains about the type of woman 'who is fit for nothing
but to sit in her drawing-room like a doll-Madonna in her
shrine'.[6]

For many reasons, then, the Romulus association is
contradictory and unstable as the sign of a woman's epic
role. The name can refer not only to the positive side of the
founding of Rome, but also to the circumstances of Romulus' birth and rise to power, a narrative of violent patriarchal
struggle. Romulus, it should be remembered, was one of
the twin sons of Rea Silvia, a woman whose uncle had
appointed her as a Vestal Virgin so that she would not
produce offspring who might usurp his power. Romulus'
father, who seduced Rea Silvia, was Mars, the god of war
and former patron of Florence. Romulus' founding of Rome
was accomplished by murder and destruction, and his
famous ploy to bring stability to the city was the rape of
Sabine women, who eventually defended their attackers and
effected an alliance between the Romans and the Sabine
men. This narrative, in which the idealised virgin Rea Silvia
is used to preserve male power, recalls Romola's position in
Florence, where men call her 'Madonna' and carry the
Virgin in devout processions that celebrate their own hegemony. The vicious power struggles recall both the warring
religious orders of Florence and the history of Romola's
own Bardi family, whose houses were sacked in the middle
of the fourteenth century in retaliation for their grasping
economic tactics. And the rape of the Sabine women recalls
the position of Romola and the other women in the novel: in
this patriarchal culture, their bodies are objects that bond
men.

Even the novel's Comtean context brings into question
the value of Romola's idealisation in the plague-village
scenes, for it is here that she most resembles the Comtean

banner of the young woman holding a male child. This secularised Madonna figure has a position in Comtean thinking very close to that of the Virgin Mary in Catholic doctrine: not as an image of female power, but as an object of inspiration for men. In Comte's scheme, the elevation of women made them unequal to men; private worship – of which the figures of mother, wife and daughter were the objects – was possible for men only. If Romola's name and position as Madonna suggest both her elevation and her powerlessness, so too does the novel's Epilogue. She is, on the one hand, the head of a female family, and such a unit suggests the possibility of escaping patriarchal hegemony. The family members do, moreover, seem happier than heretofore: Monna Brigida is content to abandon the vulgar trappings she had worn to attract men now that she has Romola as a daughter and Tessa's children to replace her dead twins; Tessa and the children have for the first time a prosperous and stable life; and Romola herself, finally freed from Tito, has a fulfilling calling.

The subversion associated with the gender plot is not absent from the novel's conclusion, however. Though Romola appears to be in a position of moral authority, she remains the conduit of language rather than a user of it, as she passes on to Tito's son the learning she received from her father and instructs him in how to be the great statesman Petrarch had hoped would bring a new life to Italy. The reference to Petrarch is telling: Eliot had once made a note in her *Commonplace Book* about 'Petrarch's contempt of women',[7] and he is also the only non-classical writer admired by the misogynistic Bardo. The reader will know, moreover, since the Medicis returned to power just three years after the novel's conclusion in 1509, that Romola's moral development did not feminise the course of history in the way that the positivists thought the Religion of Humanity would: patriarchal values, if they had been threatened at all, were eventually restored to their dominant position. Neither

does the future of the next generation appear to accord with
the new values Romola has learned. Lillo sits near 'the wide
doorway that opened on to the loggia' and entertains restless
dreams of masculine power, while Ninna, who at the age of
thirteen is at the brink of womanhood, sits in a 'narrow
inner room' making wreaths for Savonarola's altar.

It is significant, too, that the reference to Ninna's tending
the altar follows immediately after the account in the
previous chaper, entitled 'The Last Silence', of Savonarola's
execution and passage 'into eternal silence' (72). For,
ironically, it has consistently been Savonarola's *silence after
speech*, not simply the speech itself, that has sustained his
hypnotic influence. This effect is first described in the
chapter depicting Savonarola's address in the Duomo:

> Savonarola's voice had been rising in impassioned force
> up to this point, when he became suddenly silent, let his
> hands fall and clasped them quietly before him. His silence,
> instead of being the signal for small movements amongst
> his audience, seemed to be as strong a spell to them as
> his voice. Through the vast area of the cathedral men and
> women sat with faces upturned, like breathing statues, till
> the voice was heard again in clear low tones. (24)

The mesmerism effected by this silence after speech also
operates in the chapter where Savonarola persuades Romola to
return to Florence, which ends with this sentence: 'Savonarola stretched out his hands over her; but feeling would no
longer pass through the channel of speech, and he was silent'
(40). The power of Savonarola's silence over Romola then
extends into the empty space between this chapter and the
next, entitled 'Coming Back', which begins with these words:

> 'Rise, my daughter,' said Fra Girolamo at last. 'Your
> servant is waiting not far off with the mules. It is time
> that I should go onward to Florence.'

Romola arose from her knees. That silent attitude had been a sort of sacrament to her, confirming the state of yearning passivity on which she had newly entered. (41)

Here the phrase 'at last' indicates to the reader that a long silence has filled the space between the two chapters, during which Savonarola has stood with arms stretched over the kneeling Romola – 'confirming' his influence. Similarly, the contiguity of the chapter describing Savonarola's 'Last Silence' and of the Epilogue immediately following, with its references to his altar, implies not a permanent silencing, but its opposite: an 'eternal' extension of his hypnotic power, made visible in the altar to his memory. Savonarola's silence is the speaking voice of patriarchy.

In these terms, the Epilogue of *Romola* contains in its seemingly happy closure a radical negation of many of the expectations that the plot had generated. Here Ninna's position is no different from that of Romola herself as she grew up in the shadow of her brother Dino – or, for that matter, from that of Maggie Tulliver. This repetition within Romola's matriarchal family of the patriarchal power structure that fostered her own oppression thus denies the reader the satisfaction of any neatly teleological reading of the gender plot. The subordinate position of Ninna – whose mother had repeatedly lamented that neither Tito *nor Romola* was interested in her as they were in Lillo – remains in this novel, which speaks so eloquently for woman's education, a troubling detail. The conventional plot of human and historical progression reaches its predictable closure, but the desires constructed by the gender plot remain unsatisfied – muted by a silent patriarchal voice.

Felix Holt, the Radical, the novel that follows *Romola*, contains within its conventional closure a similarly unsatisfying conclusion to the gender plot. Here too women are silenced, while the male voice of Felix Holt extends even beyond the narrative's conclusion into his later 'Address to

Working Men' (published by Blackwood in *Maga* in 1868).
On the surface, however, the two narratives are quite
different from each other. While *Romola*'s historical plot is
extensively distanced in place and time – thus allowing Eliot
the occasion for extremities in action that would not be
permissible in one of her 'provincial fictions – *Felix Holt*,
set in England immediately following the passage of the first
Reform Bill in 1832, represents a return to the kinds of
conservative romance plotting that characterised *Adam
Bede* and *Silas Marner*. Like those earlier narratives, this
novel is named after its hero and ends in a traditional
patriarchal marriage. *Holt*, indeed, as several critics have
noted, contains the most politically conservative of Eliot's
plots: its supposedly radical hero opposes the enfranchise-
ment of workers, calling instead for a change in consciousness that would be achieved chiefly by the education of their
sons. Moreover, in spite of Holt's freedom in the end to
open a school and thus to work toward his aim of ex-
panding the minds of the working class, the narrative offers
no suggestion in its closure that any progress has been made
toward solving the social problems of industrial England.
There is thus a disturbing incongruity between, on the one
hand, the narrator's account in the Introduction of a
poverty so oppressive that it divides families and, on the
other hand, the vague references in the novel's conclusion to
a happy family life enjoyed by Esther and Felix in a
condition of poverty they have chosen. The novel raises
issues, in short, that its romance closure conspicuously
evades.

As is suggested by Felix's interest in educating sons and
not daughters (an alarming theory in a protagonist constructed by the creator of Maggie Tulliver and Romola),
the gender plot in *Felix Holt* is as evasive as the political plot
about the mechanisms for accomplishing change. Just as
Holt endorses restricting the power of workers to indirect
influence on politicians, so he sees the ideal woman as one

who by her influence makes 'a man's passion for her rush in one current with all the great aims of *his* life' (27: italics added). The gender plot's closure is reached, therefore, not by a formal education of boys leading to a revolution in consciousness, but by the informal education and 'inward revolution' (49) of Esther Lyon as she learns to be, in Holt's words, a woman 'whose beauty makes a great task easier to men instead of turning them away from it' (27). In choosing Holt over Harold Transome, Esther rejects her earlier romantic notions about rising in class through marriage, but this alliance also dramatises the fact that the only means for her to embrace a heroic lot lies in acquiring a husband with 'great aims' like her own, who can function in the public world on her behalf. As the narrator comments, giving voice in free indirect discourse to Esther's own thoughts,

> After all, she was a woman, and could not make her own lot. As she had once said to Felix, 'A woman must choose meaner things, because only meaner things are offered to her.' Her lot is made for her by the love she accepts. (43)

This reference to the woman's lot is ironically qualified, moreover, by its relationship with the story of the biblical Esther, whose intervention with her husband, King Ahasuerus, to spare the Jewish people from their lot to die on a determined day, was celebrated as *Purim*, the feast of lots. Unlike the Jewish people, who because of Esther's efforts could change the date of their own planned extermination to a day for the destruction of their enemies, Esther Lyon cannot reverse her unalterable lot, which is determined by her gender.

Esther is, in fact, as much a commodity in the marriage market as Romola. It is Felix himself who tells her, in words echoing those of Bernardo del Nero about Romola, 'But remember you have cost a great price – don't throw what is precious away (45). The narrator, too, implies that Esther's position is that of mediating object between men. When her inappropriateness for the single state is described, the reader is told that she was '"a fair divided excellence, whose fulness of perfection" must be in marriage'. This reference from Shakespeare's *King John* (II.i.439–40) seems superficially to elevate Esther's need for completion in marriage, but its full context casts her position in an ironic light: the quoted words are uttered by a spokesman for the disputed city of Angiers as he seeks to prevent a military conflict between England and France by offering Lady Blanch of Spain as bride to Lewis the Dauphin of France. The marriage he proposes, in other words, is not a love match but an alliance between political powers. Unlike Lady Blanch, of course, Esther at least has the freedom to choose between suitors, but in either marriage she will play the role of a passive agent enabling masculine success: if she marries Harold, she will wed him to the fortune and position of power he had for so long thought to be his own; if she marries Felix, she will subordinate her life entirely to his cause. In spite of its conservative plotting, however – and partly because of it – the narrative of *Felix Holt* as a whole raises serious questions about the very values that bring its conventional structure to a happy termination. This is true first because its major subplot – the Transome story, which preceded the Felix Holt plot in Eliot's design for the novel and which has struck many readers as more powerfully present than the relationship of Felix and Esther – constantly interrogates the premises of the romance plot. The novel is a continual dialogue of conflicting plots, and the triumph of one over the others at the end never successfully suppresses the stories that are made subordinate.

The most obvious opposing plots in *Felix Holt* take the form of two pairings: the public plot of political radicalism involving both Felix Holt and Harold Transome versus the private plot of Esther Lyon's courtship by both these men;

and the romance plot of Esther Lyon versus that of Arabella
Transome. In the first case, the public plot reaches no
resolution at all – the narrator is coolly ironic in the
Epilogue about political change in North Loamshire – and
it is finally subsumed, after Esther's testimony at Felix's
trial, by the private plot that culminates in the marriage of
Esther and Felix. In the second case, Esther's romance plot
achieves the conventionally happy closure that is denied to
Mrs Transome, but the narrator's sympathies run counter
to the assumptions created by such a narrative structure.
This opposition is first established in the novel's Introduction, where the narrator reports in free indirect discourse
the account by the coachman Mr Sampson of the Transome
story: 'As for Mr. Transome, he was as poor, half-witted a
fellow as you'd wish to see; but *she* was master, had come of
a high family, and had a spirit – you might see it in her eye
and the way she sat her horse.' Like Colonel Townley in
Adam Bede and the Spirit of the Age in *Romola*, Sampson –
whose name suggests male vulnerability in the face of
female power – has an exclusively masculine perspective
that is countered and supplemented by the narrator's different point of view. Sampson's crude perception of Mrs
Transome as usurping male authority and his snide allusion
to the 'fine stories' that might be told about her thus give
way to the narrator's 'parable' about the 'noiseless' pain
imaged in the underwold forests of the *Aeneid* and the
Inferno:

> The thorn-bushes there, and the thick-barked stems, have
> human histories hidden in them; the power of unuttered
> cries dwells in the passionless-seeming branches, and the
> red warm blood is darkly feeding the quivering nerves of
> a sleepless memory that watches through all dreams.

As if to flesh out the 'parable', this passage is immediately
followed by the description in Chapter 1 of Mrs Transome's

silent pain as she awaits the son she hopes will effect for her
a queenly metamorphosis. This view of Arabella Transome,
not the callous and threatened perspective of Sampson,
dominates the narrator's treatment of her.

This sympathetic attitude on the part of the narrator runs
counter not only to Sampson's vulgar summarising but also
to the crude nemesis of the plot itself, which rewards Esther
with marriage for her growth toward selflessness, while
punishing Mrs Transome for her failed attempts to dominate by making her powerless with both her former lover and
her son. The plot basically demonstrates that women who
seek power for themselves will suffer, while self-serving
men like Maurice Christian or John Johnson can find
prosperity and happiness in spite of their dishonest tactics.
The narrator, however, in direct contrast to the assumptions underlying the retribution of the plot, is tight-lipped
and ironic about those who are in the end rewarded, while
identifying and sympathising with the feminine powerlessness and suffering which the plot has presented as natural
and justified. Very little is said, in fact, about Esther's
marriage, except that she 'has never repented' the decision
and that there is 'a young Felix' very like his father – hardly
evidence of a satisfying closure to the gender plot. Neither
Mrs Transome nor Mrs Holt, it should be remembered,
finds happiness in her son, and the narrator has emphasised
that 'mothers have a self larger than their maternity' (8). At
the end of *Felix Holt*, the question of what has happened to
Esther's 'larger' self after her marriage is thus left largely
indeterminate. What evidence does exist from her courtship
with Felix suggests, moreover, that her sense of identity is
based entirely on him. At one point she had pondered – in
words ironically echoing Becky Sharp of Thackeray's *Vanity
Fair* on the subject of £5,000 a year – that if 'she might have
married Felix Holt, she could have been a good woman. She
felt no trust that she could ever be good without him' (32).
And when in the last chapter she finally accepts Felix, she

exclaims, 'I am weak – my husband must be greater and nobler than I am'. Esther may be presented at the end of *Felix Holt* as finding the greatest happiness a woman can achieve, but at the same time that fulfilment is exposed as limited by and dependent upon the stature of her husband.

In these terms, Mrs Transome's opposite fate can similarly be seen as resulting from her choice of mates. Her marriage to Transome, made for money, produces only an 'imbecile son' (1) and a life of isolation on an estate that has effectively become her prison. Her affair with Jermyn, an attempt to have the romantic relationship absent in her marriage, produces a son who she expects will 'give unity to her life' (1), but who eventually becomes the chief source of her misery. Imagining that Harold will be her means of communication with the world of action – exactly the role that Esther gives to Felix – she finds her son to be only the agent of her own exclusion and silencing. Significantly, the narrator treats this situation, which at the level of plot seems to be a just retribution, with intense sympathy. One of her angry outbursts at Harold invites these comments:

> She, poor woman, knew quite well that she had been unwise, and that she had been making herself disagreeable to Harold to no purpose. But half the sorrows of women would be averted if they could repress the speech they know to be useless; nay, the speech they have resolved not to utter. (2)

After Harold loses the election, the narrator again describes Mrs Transome giving voice to her sense of grievance and thus 'helping, with feminine self-defeat, to exclude herself more completely from any consultation with him. In this way poor women, whose power lies solely in their influence, make themselves like music out of tune, and only move men to run away' (34). In both these cases, as elsewhere, the narrator's comments about Mrs Transome move quickly into generalised laments about the fate of 'poor women' who are excluded from the world of men whether they speak or not. Punished by the plot for her past sins, she is held up by the narrator as an emblem of female powerlessness and anguish.

It could be argued that Esther's fate, in which she saves Felix by speaking out at his trial, contradicts the narrator's pronouncements about female speech. The fact remains, however, that Esther strengthens Felix's case only by pleasing the 'good fathers' of the court with her 'maidenly fervour'. As Sir Maximus Debarry remarks, 'The girl made me cry' (47); and Harold makes a similar point when he tells Esther, 'You made all the men wish what you wished' (49). Esther's voice holds sway in the masculine court, in other words, only because its patriarchs have smiled upon her; unable to break through the structures of masculine hegemony, Esther succeeds, like her biblical namesake, merely by pleasing the men who exercise power. In this sense, her life is not altogether different from Mrs Transome's, though she succeeds where Arabella fails: both women must seek access to the world through men, and neither can act without male endorsement and sponsorship.

Such similarity between apparently contrasting characters operates not only in the case of Esther and Mrs Transome, but also in the analogous case of Felix and Harold, both of whom aggressively attempt to subdue women. Harold vows not to marry again because 'English wives . . . want to give their opinions about everything' and 'interfere with a man's life' (1), but he is then attracted to Esther because she appears tameable and would offer a solution to his financial problems. Felix vows not to marry because a woman would interfere with his noble purpose, but is drawn to Esther because he wants to taunt her for her vanity and hence to 'change' her for his own purposes: '"A Peacock!" thought Felix. "I should like to come and scold her every day, and make her cry and cut her fine hair off"'

(5). As if unconsciously to turn his opprobrium back upon himself, Felix links Esther's presumed faults with the peacock – a male emblem of vanity like the turkey-cock that is mocked in the motto for the chapter describing the joke played by Scales on the vain Maurice Christian: 'it spreads its tail in self-glorification, but shows you the wrong side of that ornament – liking admiration, but knowing not what is admirable' (12). The text thus indirectly links Esther's female vanity with that of the males, including Felix himself.

Felix also bears some resemblance to Harold in his past relationship with women. While Harold has bought a wife (or mistress) in the East, Felix has based his conversion to virtue on the 'six weeks' debauchery' in Scotland he vaguely describes to Rufus Lyon. Though he is not explicit about any associations with women during this time, he mentions, as one of the temptations he finally overcame, 'old women breathing gin as they passed me on the stairs – wanting to turn my life into easy pleasure' (5). Before meeting Esther, in other words, both Harold and Felix have viewed prostitution as a means of enjoying women's bodies without being subject to their wills and desires. In response to his past, Felix has chosen a more virtuous course than Harold, that of a difficult chastity, but he also displays an antagonism toward women that matches Harold's cold contempt:

> I could grind my teeth at such self-satisfied minxes, who think they can tell everybody what is the correct thing, and the utmost stretch of their ideas will not place them on a level with the intelligent fleas. I should like to see if she could be made ashamed of herself. (5)

Felix is responding to the potential in Esther to be the kind of wife that Rosamond Vincy is to Lydgate in *Middlemarch* (although there is no real evidence that she will become such a person). The violence of his response, however, as the peacock image also suggests, seems to involve a projection on to the woman of something he fears in himself.

Harold and Felix are not the only men who desire to subdue women. Their attitudes are literalised in the cameo portrait of Dredge, who beats his wife because 'if she jabbers at me, I can't abide it' (11). And a more refined version of the same impulse appears in the repulsive Matthew Jermyn, whose 'mere brute strength of a masculine creature [rebels]' against the words of Mrs Transome: 'He felt almost inclined to throttle the voice out of this woman' (43). In these aggressive feelings toward his former mistress, as well as in his habitual swindling from her estate, Jermyn exposes the real basis for the stereotype of the 'soft-glancing, versifying young' romantic hero he once was (47).

Even the mild and virtuous Rufus Lyon shares with the other male characters in the novel a resistance to the female voice and a conviction that women will interfere with the important aims of his life. From the first scene in which Lyon appears, he is presented as impatient with his 'weak sisters', Mary Holt and Lyddy, whose 'relief of *groaning*' at their unhappiness he cannot tolerate – this in spite of the fact that he is described by the narrator in the same scene as speaking 'aloud, *groaningly*', about his difficulty in accepting the faults of women (4: italics added). This tendency to blame women for a fault he shares with them seems especially ironic in view of Lyon's past history with Esther's mother, described in a subplot that Eliot decided to insert into *Felix Holt* after she had begun working on the novel. Like Felix, Lyon regards his attraction to a woman as moral backsliding, a sensual distraction that draws him away from his 'argumentative conquest on the side of right'. The narrator makes clear, moreover, that what Lyon fears from his 'worship' of Annette Ledru is her interference not only with his moral mission but also with his 'personal ambition'.

What the story finally reveals, however, is that Annette's sacrifice for Lyon turns out to be greater than his for her.

Though he loses his position as 'the admired pastor of a large Independent congregation' after taking in the destitute woman and her child, Annette herself repays him – in spite of the fact that she feels no more attraction to him than does Tina for the worshipping Gilfil or Maggie Tulliver for the similarly adoring Philip Wakem – by marrying him. Her decision is presented by the narrator as a recognition that the sensuous pleasures of her life have disappeared. She says to Lyon, 'J'aimais les fleurs, les bals, la musique, et mon mari qui était beau. But all that is gone away.' Annette's final fate, then, is much like Tina's: having denied her own desire in order to satisfy the man who wants to 'call her his own' – a suppression which in this case includes the forfeiture of her mother tongue – she retreats into the passivity and death that so often beset those women in Eliot's fiction who consent to being the objects of masculine 'worship'. In presenting her decline, the narrator invokes an image, very like that used to describe Tina's withdrawal from life, of a plant that fails to thrive: 'She withered like a plant in strange air, and the three years of life that remained were but a slow and gentle death.' Though Lyon has sacrificed his ambition and his 'special work' (6) for Annette, she gives to him her sexuality and her life. She also bequeaths to him the child who continues to sustain him, just as Eppie had sustained Silas Marner. Her story makes Lyon's impatience with feminine suffering especially striking for its blindness and insensitivity.

In addition to providing an ironic context for the pervasive masculine contempt of women in *Felix Holt*, the Annette Ledru story serves as well to focus one of the novel's suppressed and unfulfilled plots: Esther's yearning for her lost mother. Like many of Eliot's characters, Esther has only fragmented memories of the lost mother and her language:

But she had no more than a broken vision of the time before she was five years old – the time when the word

oftenest on her lips was 'Mamma'; when a low voice
spoke caressing French words to her, and she in her turn
repeated the words to her rag-doll; when a very small
white hand, different from any that came after, used to
pat her, and stroke her, and tie on her frock and pinafore,
and when at last there was nothing but sitting with a doll
on a bed where mamma was lying, till her father once
carried her away. Where distinct memory began, there
was no longer the low caressing voice and the small white
hand. (6)

Esther is unable, of course, to return to this half-
remembered pre-Oedipal state, but she briefly finds a
substitute for it in her warm relationship with Arabella
Transome, which culminates in the night they spend
together after Harold has discovered who his father is.
Esther's ministrations to Arabella make up the most explicitly sexual and intimate scene in the novel:

The disordered grey hair – the haggard face – the
reddened eyelids under which the tears seemed to be
coming again with pain, pierced Esther to the heart. A
passionate desire to soothe this suffering woman came
over her. She clung round her again, and kissed her poor
quivering lips and eyelids, and laid her young cheek
against the pale and haggard one. Words could not be
quick or strong enough to utter her yearning.

Significantly, though Arabella is the one who is suffering, it
is Esther who initially feels the 'yearning' for a yielding
closeness with the older woman and asks if she can undress
her. 'I shall seem to have a mother again,' she implores. 'Do
let me' (50). This apotheosis of female closeness is only
temporary, however, for Esther's rejection of Harold and
acceptance of Felix require a turning away from the new
mother and a return to the father: just as Esther had been

carried away from her mother's deathbed by her father, so she leaves Mrs Transome's bed of suffering – in a sense the older woman's deathbed, since she does not emerge again in the narrative until her death is passingly mentioned in the Epilogue – to return to Rufus Lyon. The only sustained closeness between women finally permitted in the novel is that between Arabella and her loyal Denner, who had been banished by her mistress the night that Esther came to her. Left alone with her son, Arabella returns to the temporarily displaced Denner, the single person who has consistently loved her and listened to her embittered voice. This relationship – itself a kind of marriage in which Arabella plays a patriarchal role – receives little attention in the novel's closure, however, as the narrator reverts, with Esther, back to the father and to the romance plot.

Esther's movement away from Arabella is, of course, necessary, for she can stay with this potential mother figure only by marrying the selfish and tyrannical Harold. In terms of narrative structure, however, the fact that the romance plot displaces the plot of yearning for the lost mother is itself significant. In the conclusion of Charlotte Brontë's *Shirley*, Caroline Helstone had enjoyed both types of fulfilment, but Eliot's narrative puts the two types of plot in a relationship of binary opposition: the patriarchal plot dominates the maternal plot, leaving it only the power of expressing its own exclusion. The suppression of the maternal plot is made all the more emphatic, moreover, by the parallel and less necessary banishment of still another potential mother from Esther's married life. The Epilogue reports that Rufus Lyon 'joined [Esther and Felix] where they dwelt', while Mrs Holt, whose groaning had made Lyon so impatient, remained behind in Treby Magna. Esther's marriage thus effects the union of her father and husband, while excluding the maternal figure whose presence threatens to disrupt the patriarchal household. The mother–daughter relationship – brought so vividly to the reader's consciousness in the chapters dealing with Esther's feelings about both Annette Ledru and Mrs Transome – is ruthlessly excluded from the narrative resolution of *Felix Holt*. The plots of female desire, however, are not altogether absent from the novel's closure, for their powerful presence in the earlier sections of the narrative cannot help but draw attention to the failure of the romance structure to accommodate their completion. Like the plot of political radicalism, these unresolved plots stand out visibly in the overdetermined closure of *Felix Holt*, all the more conspicuous for having been suppressed.

The tension in *Felix Holt* between plots of masculine and feminine desire is exacerbated, as in *Romola*, by the novel's explicitly historical perspective, which renders the position of women particularly problematic: if women have a role in the private but not the public sphere, while men have a role in both, then gender automatically creats a radical imbalance in any plot that attempts to move toward a reconciliation of the private and the public. In conventional historical fiction, in other words, there is little space for plots of feminine desire that move away from the standard courtship narrative. This fact may well account for the intense ambivalence of the conclusion of *Romola*, where although the heroine has lived beyond courtship and marriage – and, indeed, has briefly assumed a role of public leadership – she is seen in the end perpetuating the traditions that have oppressed her. *Felix Holt*, perhaps because it represents a return to a nineteenth-century British context, contains a plot that is more conservative still in its insistence that female desire can be satisfied and expressed only within marriage. *The Spanish Gypsy*, a narrative poem which Eliot began to write after the completion of *Romola* and to which she returned after finishing *Felix Holt*, addresses even more explicitly the difficulty for a woman of reconciling private and public roles. Its historical plot – set in late fifteenth-century Spain where Moors, Jews and Gypsies joined forces against persecution by the Catholic Inquisition – allowed Eliot, as in *Romola*, to place her heroine in a more extreme position than those of her 'provincial' heroines and to explore the contradictions that emerge when a woman embraces a public role in a patriarchal culture.

The Spanish Gypsy appears to embody a feminist plot that both *Romola* and *Felix Holt* negate or repress: unlike Romola, Fedalma becomes a leader of her own people; unlike Esther Lyon, she rejects marriage in order to assume her public role. What the narrative ultimately reveals, however, is that both Fedalma's possible choices involve the subordination of her desire to masculine prerogative. A parallel situation exists in the narrative's presentation of the exploitation by Spanish Christianity of alien races and cultures: sexism, racism and imperialism are exposed as part of the same power structure, one that simultaneously exploits and demonises all that is different from itself.

Fedalma is an especially complex focus for the narrative's treatment of power relations. As the poem's title suggests, she brings together attributes that are generally mutually exclusive: a Gypsy by birth, she is a Spaniard in her cultural background and thus has the choice of inhabiting either world, that of the dominators or that of the dominated. Her gender makes this double identity all the more complicated: though she has roots in both cultures, she must also occupy a subordinate position in whichever one she chooses, for both her lover Don Silva and her father Zarca share the same view of her as commodity. This assumption is more apparent, of course, in Don Silva, who even attempts to buy Fedalma from Zarca and whose erotic address to her is the acquisitive word 'Mine!' Thus Fedalma's chief hope for her marriage is that she will have the power, like Queen Esther, to influence her husband in the direction of good. Zarca, on the other hand, appears at the outset to represent an alternative to Don Silva's patriarchal values: as a member of a dark and outcast race, he is associated, like women, with repression by patriarchy. He also, unlike Don Silva, appears to be inviting Fedalma to assume a position of authority in her tribe. The terms of the invitation, however – like Felix Holt's proposal to Esther that she join *his* cause – still privilege Zarca's desire over Fedalma's: to be Don Silva's 'Duchess' or Zarca's 'Queen' is to act in service to a masculine will. Zarca's influence over Fedalma is ultimately very like Savonarola's over Romola. At his death, we are told, 'He spoke the parting prayer that was command, / Must sway her will, and *reign invisibly*' (Book 4: italics added). Like Savonarola's eternal silence that extends his hypnotic influence after his death, this final speech by Zarca transforms Fedalma into the eternal 'priestess' at his 'altar-step', one who makes her body his 'funeral urn' and places 'death above desire' (Book 5) in pursuit of a cause that she knows to be futile without his physical presence.

Fedalma's final powerlessness as Zarca's avatar makes the conclusion of *The Spanish Gypsy*, which might otherwise have been construed as a happy resolution to a plot of female vocation, brutally ironic: having chosen to act through her father rather than through a husband, Fedalma finds herself governing a people who cannot respond to her leadership because she is a woman. Her final position is not that of a female leader, but rather that of the submissive figure that inspired Eliot to write Fedalma's story in the first place: Mary assenting to the Father's will at the Annunciation. Images of the Madonna's life permeate the accounts of Fedalma's relationship with her father. The word 'pregnant' is used several times in reference to the role he asks her to fill, and her leadership of the Zincali is presented more than once as a type of motherhood. At his death, Zinca reinforces the idea of Fedalma as a bearer of the saviour rather than as a saving figure in her own right: 'My daughter, lay your arm / Beneath my head . . . so . . . bend and breathe on me.' In this self-choreographed Gypsy Pieta, Zinca makes himself the compositional centre of the picture, thus establishing – like Savonarola, he does this through his 'silence' – that his influence will extend even beyond his physical death. If Fedalma can assume with Don Silva only Queen Esther's mediating and prostituting role, with Zarca she must remain, like the Madonna, only the saviour's conduit. As in *Romola* and *Felix Holt*, a seemingly satisfying closure is thus undercut by details that call it into question. All three of Eliot's most explicitly historical fictions – whether they are set in fifteenth-century Europe or in the England of 1832 – ultimately place her heroines in the same position: in ways that suit their different historical contexts, Romola, Esther Lyon, and Fedalma all serve only as agents of masculine authority. Eliot's use of the genre of historical fiction, even when she distances the action from Victorian England, exposes the anomalous position of woman's desire in a form that seeks to reconcile the public and private spheres.

6 Poetry and the Late Novels: Fictions of Diffused Desire

In the years after the publication of *The Spanish Gypsy*, Eliot was writing shorter poems and poetic dramas which allowed her to experiment further in her treatment of female roles. While the conventions of realistic fiction had generally confined her to plots of courtship and personal development, the form and subject matter of various poetic genres allowed Eliot to explore female aspiration in a series of new and different contexts. In 1869 alone, the year when she began work on *Middlemarch*, she wrote five poems, all of which in some way celebrate a transforming feminine power that is not entirely dependent on marriage. 'Agatha', a pastoral treatment of simple heroism along the lines of Wordsworth's 'Michael', praises spinsterhood and singles out its nurturing role in the rural community. The poem celebrates a feminine power that is repeatedly and emphatically distinguished from the masculine. Just as in the opening lines the hilly maternal landscape displaces the reader's presumed expectations of a paternal sublime 'where rocks / Soar harsh above the troops of hurrying pines', and just as Agatha's habitation of Sanct Märgen follows that of the 'Tall-frocked and cowled' monks, so Agatha's love is singled out as 'willing but not omnipotent' and therefore different from that of the 'dread power' holding sway over life and death. In 'Agatha', a love that is maternal without being defined by biological motherhood exceeds in its benevolence the omnipotence of the Christian masculine god.

While 'Agatha' celebrates the status of the old maid, 'How Lisa Loved the King' singles out for praise a young maiden's passionate adulation of her king and his graceful response to it. Taking a story from Boccaccio that emphasises sexual competition, Eliot constructs the narrative as a fairy tale and presents Lisa's love of the king – in answer to the riddle of the poem's title – not as a sexual yearning, but as a 'transformed desire' for the sphere of action defined as masculine in chivalric culture. Like Desdemona listening to Othello's adventures, Lisa is unable herself to perform heroic deeds and so projects her own desires for great action on to the man who, by virtue of his class and gender, can act for her in the struggle against evil. The happy closure of Lisa's fairy tale is thus accomplished, not by a sexual union with the already married king, but by the king's willingness to cross class lines in order to visit her, by his recognition of her devotion, and – most significantly – by his promise always to carry her colours into battle. In exchange for this representation in the sphere of heroic action, Lisa agrees to obey the king's request that she marry the loving Perdicone. Appropriately, King Pedro – using the authoritative royal 'We' – presents this marriage as a means for Lisa to pay service to her country: 'We must not wrong yourself and Sicily / By letting all your blooming years pass by / Unmated: you will give the world its due / From beauteous maiden and become a matron true.' This closure clearly satisfies the generic requirement that all the good figures live happily ever after, but it simultaneously exposes the limitations of female happiness in a chivalric world: here a woman's desire for heroic action can be satisfied only indirectly, through male representation, and the single means by which she can pay her country 'its due' is to marry.

Woman's indirect access to the masculine sphere of action is also a central subject in Eliot's series of eleven sonnets entitled 'Brother and Sister'. The sonnets are like 'Tintern

Abbey' and *The Prelude* in their emphasis on the influence of early memory, but they reverse some basic Wordsworthian assumptions: here the sister–brother relationship is more important than that between self and nature,[1] and the sister's point of view problematises Wordsworth's use of Dorothy as silent audience and muse. In these poems a female voice, like that of a Maggie Tulliver who survives to maturity, herself speaks, reminiscing about both her childhood affection for her brother and her perception of his superior status, that of a man in relation to his dog.

The poems are an exploration of the contrasting lessons that the brother and sister take into adulthood; the boy learns to broaden his own sphere of action by sympathetically moderating his sense of power over his less privileged sister; the girl learns her own inability to control what happens to her, even when her fate is a happy one. This is illustrated in the story of the fishing trip, in which the sister provokes an angry cry in her brother for forgetting to watch for barges while holding the rod, only to find, simultaneously, that she has hooked a silver perch. Her 'guilt' is consequently turned to 'merit', and the girl child comes to learn the arbitrariness of success – that 'luck [is] with glory wed'. In contrast to the boy's lesson, which confirms his own importance in the scheme of things, the girl thus learns her inconsequence in the world. This perception, however, is also presented as the basis for the speaker's role as artist: 'Those long days measured by my little feet / Had chronicles which yield me many a text; / Where irony still finds an image meet / Of full-grown judgements in this world perplext.' To have feminine 'little feet' rather than a masculine 'larger tread' (a punning reference to the metre of the sonnets, as well as to the speaker's girlhood) thus entails a feeling of powerlessness, but it also gives to the woman an ironic perspective, a voice, and a text.

'Stradivarius', another poem written in 1869, is not about a female character, but it deals none the less with the relationship of the artist to subordinate roles. Written in the style of a dialogue by Robert Browning, the poem contains an argument between Antonio Stradivari, maker of the famous violins, and Naldo, 'a painter of eclectic school' who challenges Stradivari's commitment to his craft. Naldo embraces an idea of impulsive romantic genius which is dependent on a Byronic style of life and a resulting 'influence' in the market-place. Stradivari, however, rejects such macho image-peddling, claiming that he has been chosen 'to help' God by making violins. A much more extreme version of Fra Lippo Lippi's assertion in Browning's poem that God 'uses' artists by 'lending [their] minds out' (305–6), Stradivari's argument suggests that God is incomplete without the services of the violin-maker. Significantly, Stradivari links his work, not with a masculine ideal of genius like Naldo's but with patient feminine nurturing: 'If thou wilt call thy pictures eggs / I call the hatching, Work'. The poem's narrator, moreover, associates Stradivari's 'strong' language with a feminine voice. In answer to the impertinent questions of his neighbours, the violin-maker invokes 'Fact', personified in the poem as a 'gnomic, cutting, or ironical' female speaker. Like the 'Brother and Sister' poems, 'Stradivarius' thus elevates both feminine craftmanship and the discourse used to defend it: an ironic woman's voice.

At the end of 1869, while Eliot was nursing the dying Thornton Lewes, she wrote another poem about a male artist figure whose creations are linked to a feminine image. 'The Legend of Jubal', referred to by Lewes as 'a myth of [Eliot's] own creation' (*GEL* 5: 205), extends the story of Cain and Abel beyond its biblical boundaries, supplementing it with a narrative about the birth of music. As Mary Wilson Carpenter has pointed out, this revision of the creation story 'cancels the misogynistic implications of the biblical myth'[2] and locates the fall not in Eve's temptation of Adam but in Cain's descendants. The poem revises the biblical redemption myth as well: instead of a story about the sacrifice of a god-man, Eliot creates a narrative recounting the dangers of religious enthusiasm and the redemptive qualities of music for its mortal creator. Jubal's creative acts, moreover, are continually associated with female reproduction and nurturing: his technique of blending the sounds of nature and of men is compared to a pregnancy, and his artistic aims are similarly presented as an unborn creature calling out not only for birth but also for a lifetime of nurturing. Jubal's death is then presented as a return to the earth-mother, the only figure who recognises him in his old age. In his acts of artistic creation, Jubal thus mothers and is mothered. 'The Legend of Jubal', like 'Stradivarius', identifies the role of the artist, not with masculine insemination, but with the feminine roles of bearing and nurturing.

'Armgart', a poetic drama in five scenes written in 1870, continues to focus on the role of the artist, but – like *Middlemarch*, which Eliot was composing at the same time – it treats as well the problematic relationship of human aspiration with gender. 'Armgart' reveals, in fact, that while an association with feminine roles seems to strengthen such male artists as Stradivarius and Jubal, the same does not hold true for the woman who seeks to create beauty. Armgart's story is thus an exploration of various female roles and their relationship to the aspirations of the woman artist. At the beginning, Armgart is presented as a singer of opera who possesses 'Caesar's ambition' and who 'subdues' her listeners with the power of her voice and talent. These conventionally masculine attributes make Armgart highly successful as an artist and protect her from woman's standard position as commodity. Indeed, although she is courted by the devoted Graf Dornberg, Armgart rejects his proposal of marriage – even after her debate with him about women's roles, in which he finally agrees to allow her to continue her artistic career – because, as she tells him, 'Your silent tolerance would torture me, / And on that rack

I should deny the good / I yet believed in' (2). With this allusion to the hidden violence of passive tolerance, Armgart effectively rejects the happy closure that had concluded *Aurora Leigh*, Elizabeth Barrett Browning's poem about the female artist, in which the hero learns before his marraige to accept his wife's art. In Eliot's fictions, there is never any happy conjunction for women of the love plot and the plot of artistic aspiration.

The rejection of the *Aurora Leigh* closure seems all the more striking in the latter scenes of Eliot's poem, where Armgart is rendered '*speechless*' by the loss of her singing voice. A natural expectation at this point would certainly be that without her voice Armgart could still find satisfaction in marriage to the man who had loved her even before her artistic success. Dornberg does not reappear at this point, however, except in his letter to Armgart, which reveals that his love for her had depended on the sense that she was 'lifted . . . apart' from the 'crowd' of women and on the possibility for suppression of her artistic talent as she became 'A wife with glory possible absorbed / Into her husband's actual'. Clearly, Armgart had read Dornberg's character accurately; her own fault, however, is that she relies as much as Dornberg on her own superiority over 'the crowd' of other women, and it is this reliance on a belief in her superiority that provokes the lame and unloved Walpurga to initiate the poem's second debate on women's roles. Presented from the beginning as occupying a feminine position in her relationship with Armgart – it is she who unobtrusively prepares the meal for her after the concert – Walpurga is like Lisa and the speaker of the 'Brother and Sister' sonnets in her projection of her own desires on to the larger sphere of the loved one. When Armgart loses her voice, however, Walpurga does not, like Dornberg, withdraw her love. Instead, she kisses Armgart's hands to make them warm and later, in her anger, forces Armgart to see the egotism that had been fostered in her by her masculine

position of power and privilege. Armgart's newly acquired
self-knowledge then allows her to notice the suffering of her
teacher Leo, the unheralded composer who had for so many
years projected his own desire for success on to her career.
Assuming Leo's subordinate teaching role for herself,
Armgart then resolves to move to Freiburg: 'Walpurga was
born there, / And loves the place. She quitted it for me /
These five years past. Now I will take her there / Dear Leo,
I will bury my dead joy.'

   This decision, by which Armgart returns her cousin's
feminine love and accepts her own new subordinate position, makes the closure of the poem doubly subversive of
conventional plots. First, the courtship plot gives way to a
narrative celebrating female bonding, and second, the plot
of masculine ambition gives way to a narrative of feminine
identification with the talents of another. Significantly, this
revision of the ambition plot is presented as the death of one
child and the adoption of another, and the metaphor of
maternal adoption, in turn, is clearly distinguished from
any endorsement of female subordination: it is Leo's
teaching role, after all, that Armgart is assuming, and the
voice that replaces her own is not a man's but a woman's.
The painful lesson that Armgart learns is not that women
must be subordinate to men, but that women and men alike
must, as Walpurga and Leo have done, accept and value
'their pauper's heritage'. The startling subversion of the
'Armgart' plot finally lies, therefore, in the ascendance of
Walpurga's and Leo's values over Dornberg's: the loss of
her voice finally leads Armgart, not to 'glory possible
absorbed / Into her husband's actual', but to a recognition
that glory, when it comes, is dependent on adulation from
'ruthless Nature's chary average'. Privilege and mastery are
exposed as a function not only of gender but more generally
of that which determines gender, chance itself – the 'luck'
that the speaker of the 'Brother and Sister' sonnets discovered to be 'with glory wed'. In Eliot's poetry, the mar-

riage metaphor, seen as evidence of providential design in so much nineteenth-century fiction, is used ironically to describe the arbitrariness of human lots.

The tenuous relationship of desire, luck and gender with ideas about providential marriage is explored much more extensively in *Middlemarch*, the novel that was emerging in Eliot's mind as she composed her poems about feminine roles and artist figures. As countless critics have noted, a major focus of *Middlemarch*, established in the Prelude's references to St Theresa, is the incompatibility with Victorian 'domestic reality' of female aspiration for an 'epic life'. Implicitly assuming the Darwinian language of the ongoing nineteenth-century debate about 'woman's nature', the narrator complains that there is more 'variation' among women 'than anyone would imagine from the sameness of women's coiffure and the favourite love-stories in prose and verse'.[3] The novel then explores the ways in which nineteenth-century social customs and ideas about romantic love restrict the lives of women, in spite of the variation among them. Concentrating on three women with radically different personalities and circumstances – one from the gentry, one from the rising middle class, and one from the lower middle class – the novel exposes the extent to which all of their marriages, happy or not, require the subordination of the woman's aims to those of her husband: in the middling Midlands world of Middlemarch, feminine power is always mediated by masculine representation. From the beginning, the narrator also links this analysis of gender relations to the novel's historical dimension, its concern to present 'A Study of Provincial Life'. Comparing her/his approach to that of Herodotus, who began his history with an account of the abductions of three women, this ungendered historian attempts to tell 'what had been' by using 'a woman's lot' as a 'starting-point' (11).[4] The novel's historical approach is thus clearly established as focusing on the male ownership and exchange of women: Eliot's study of 'provincial life' is a detailed presentation of patriarchal power relations and their suppression of feminine desire.

Middlemarch focuses first of all on its representative of the gentry, Dorothea Brooke, whose disastrous marriage to Edward Casaubon is presented as a Quixotic pursuit of intellectual and moral idealism. Dorothea's desire for an epic life echoes that of many of Eliot's earlier heroines: like Lisa, she projects her own ambition to fight evil on to a male who she thinks can represent her in the sphere of action; like Fedalma, she hopes that she can urge the men over whom she has influence (Chettam, for example) to perform virtuous actions; like Priscilla Lammeter, she enjoys the freedom of riding horseback and wants 'authority' in her household as well as the 'homage' that accompanies it. In these terms, her plans to build new cottages – an echo of the more elaborate architectural blueprints of Amos Barton and Sir Christopher Cheverel[5] – reflect an impulse that is as ambitious as it is charitable. This is made clear in the scene where Mr Brooks tells Dorothea of Casaubon's proposal; here Dorothea is momentarily sympathetic that 'poor Bunch' will be hanged for sheep-stealing, but immediately forgets about his fate at her uncle's mention of Casaubon. Dorothea's adulation of the old patriarch is an expression, moreover, not of her instinct for charity or of her habit of subordination but rather of her intense desire for masculine learning and power. The narrator remarks, 'it was not entirely out of devotion to her future husband that she wished to know Latin and Greek. Those provinces of masculine knowledge seemed to her a standing-ground from which all truth could be seen more truly' (7). For Dorothea, Casaubon's intellectual pursuits provide 'new vistas' on 'that toy-box history of the world adapted to young ladies which had made the chief part of her education' (10); her naive admiration for him is a response to her trivialising girlhood training.

Dorothea's strategy of acquiring masculine knowledge by

means of subordination to a powerful patriarch is eventually shown in her marriage to Casaubon to be pathetically misguided. Here the courtship plot leads not to a happy consummation of the partners' desires, but to anguishing frustration of them. As in *Romola*, the wedding is a gap in the narrative, allowing emphasis to be placed on its aftermath, the marriage itself. Significantly, the narrator returns the reader's attention to Dorothea (after eight chapters that have failed even to mention her) by alluding to her relationship with Casaubon as the last and smallest in a series of patriarchal power relationships:

> When George the Fourth was still reigning over the privacies of Windsor, when the Duke of Wellington was Prime Minister, and Mr Vincy was mayor of the old corporation of Middlemarch, Mrs Casaubon, born Dorothea Brooke, had taken her wedding journey to Rome. (19)

The exact nature of Dorothea's relationship with the patriarchal Casaubon is then only indirectly presented, in the image of her seen by Will Ladislaw as she stands vacantly staring at a streak of sunlight in front of 'the marble voluptuousness' of 'the reclining Ariadne, then called the Cleopatra' (19). Here Dorothea's lack of interest in the sensuous statue is one of many indications that her sexual life with Casaubon, whether or not he is impotent, is not a satisfying one.[6] Nor, it turns out, has her quest for masculine knowledge been worth the sexual price she had paid for it. Isolated by Casaubon from his work rather than drawn into it, Dorothea is left only with 'the gentlewoman's oppressive liberty' of filling her time with frivolous activities. As a result, she sees Rome, in a grotesque image of her own mental state, as a scene of 'stupendous fragmentariness'. The horror of this time is not obliterated, moreover, by Dorothea's later happiness in her second marriage. As the narrator points out, anticipating her future even after the novel's closure, no one 'would ever know what she thought of a wedding journey to Rome', and her nightmare vision of the place continued '*all her life*' to plague her 'in certain states of dull forlornness' (20: italics added).

An important aspect of *Middlemarch*'s critique of patriarchal marriage is its focus on the price that male as well as female characters must pay when they act out their respective gender roles. Thus while Dorothea's marriage to Casaubon fails to satisfy any of her expectations for participation in masculine power, his unhappiness in the relationship stems from his perception that she has desires separate from his own. As their first argument reveals, he is threatened at the outset by her yearning for knowledge because he fears – rightly, as it turns out – that she will discover the narrowness and futility of his scholarly pursuits. While denying Dorothea intellectual companionship, Casaubon is also afraid, as their second argument reveals, that she will seek it elsewhere. In this case, Will Ladislaw's projected visit is the contentious issue, and Casaubon argues against it even before Dorothea has ventured an opinion about it. Her angry response, 'Wait at least till I appear to consult my own pleasure apart from yours' (29), pinpoints the actual basis for their disagreement: though Dorothea has not yet allowed her desires to diverge from his, Casaubon resents even the potential in her for such an assertion of difference.

The issue of Dorothea's separate desires eventually becomes the focus in *Middlemarch* for still another exploration, like those in *Romola* and *The Spanish Gypsy*, of patriarchal power relationships that continue beyond the death of the father figure. Casaubon's fear of Dorothea's autonomous needs is so intense that he attempts to exert his power over her even further by asking her to promise that she will always 'avoid doing what I should deprecate, and apply yourself to do what I should desire' (48). His 'Dead Hand' seeks – like Savonarola's 'eternal silence' and Zarca's voice that 'went into silence' at his death – to extend his influence beyond even his own lifespan, to 'keep his cold grasp on Dorothea's life' (50). Unlike Romola and Fedalma, however, Dorothea is saved by Casaubon's death from answering his demand for submission and is able eventually to counter his mute power with her own authoritative silence. Just as she had delayed making any promises to Casaubon on the night of his death – creating 'the silence in her husband's ear' that 'was never more to be broken' (48) – so she responds to the codicil in his will forbidding her marriage to Ladislaw 'with the sense that around his last hard demand and his last injurious assertion of his power, the silence was unbroken' (50). Dorothea persists in this quiet deferral until she returns to live at Lowick, at which point her silence becomes a reproachful voice. Walking through the house, she is seen 'carrying on her thoughts as if they were a speech to be heard by her husband', and she then answers in the 'silent colloquy' of a written text Casaubon's request that she carry out his research: *Do you not see now that I could not submit my soul to yours, by working hopelessly at what I have no belief in? – Dorothea* (54).

Casaubon's demand for a promise from Dorothea that she live for his desires rather than her own appears at the time it is made to apply only to his researches. After the codicil to his will has been revealed, however, it becomes clear that the indefinite terms of the request would have included as well a claim that had never occurred to Dorothea, the injunction not to marry Ladislaw. This revelation of Casaubon's deceptiveness in his desperation to control Dorothea casts into doubt the sincerity of even his words of kindness toward her at the end of chapter 42: 'Come, my dear, come. You are young, and need not to extend your life by watching.' These words, singled out by some critics as a compelling instance of Casaubon's tenderness, need to be seen in the context of what preceded them. In this chapter, Lydgate had told Casaubon of his precarious physical condition, after which Casaubon had coldly rejected Dorothea's affectionate gestures toward him and had retreated to his study, where he remained 'much occupied' all evening. It is very possible, therefore, that it was during this time – just after he had learned that his death might be imminent – that Casaubon wrote the codicil to his will. The relief brought on by such an action might well account, then, for Casaubon's sudden change in behaviour toward the wife whose desires he fears when he cannot control them. Whether or not Casaubon wrote the codicil at this moment, moreover, it is clear that the promise he tries to exact from Dorothea, apparently with reference to his *Synoptical Tabulation*, would have held her, even more forcefully than the written words of his will, to his desire that she not marry Ladislaw. In these terms, it is significant that, as the narrator points out, underlying Dorothea's return to Lowick and her written refusal to continue the tabulation is her 'deep longing' (54) to see Will Ladislaw. Just as Casaubon had sought to draw Dorothea away from Ladislaw by exacting a promise presumed to apply only to his researches, so Dorothea, in her desire to return to Will, makes her first gesture toward seeing him by refusing to continue Casaubon's research. Dorothea's indirection here matches Casaubon's own, and the silent words of her letter to Casaubon are simply an early version of the words she will utter out loud in defiance of him when she marries Will Ladislaw.

This reading strongly suggests that Dorothea accomplishes in her marriage to Will Ladislaw a radical reversal of the submissive responses by Romola and Fedalma to the silent voices of dead paternal authorities – that in choosing him she for the first time finds her own 'will' and satisfies the desires for masculine knowledge and power that had first impelled her to marry Casaubon. As some critics have noted, Will is in many senses an ideal mate for Dorothea. With his Polish background, his resemblance to his disinherited grandmother, and his metaphoric association with gypsies, Ladislaw is generally connected with a marginalisation that also marks the feminine experience. His friendship with the kindly spinster Miss Noble, who finally orchestrates the scene in which he and Dorothea decide to marry, also links Will with the feminine sphere, making him, as Gilbert and Gubar have phrased it, 'Eliot's radically anti-patriarchal attempt to create an image of masculinity attractive to women'.[7] It is also this unconventional dimension in Ladislaw that has led many critics to attack his characterisation for its lack of conviction and manliness – for its failure, in short, to conform with the contours of the standard romance hero.

If one looks at the gender plot that runs in partial opposition to the romance plot, however, the marriage to Will Ladislaw presents problems for quite a different set of reasons. Like Philip Wakem with Maggie Tulliver, Will sees the destructiveness in Dorothea's habit of self-denial but simultaneously fails to comprehend the potential injuriousness of his own adoration of her and his perception of her as an artistic object. Rejecting Adolf Naumann's obsession with Dorothea as a pictorial image, Will, who is obsessed with her voice, merely translates her into a verbal artifice. As he tells Dorothea when she complains that she 'could never produce a poem', 'You *are* a poem – and that is to be the best part of a poet – what makes up the poet's consciousness in his best moods' (22). This reduction of Dorothea to an aesthetic object and a part of the male poet's mind – a version of Wordsworth's attitude toward his sister – is consistent with Will's continually chivalrous view of Dorothea. With his resolve to 'watch over' her even 'if he gave up everything else in life' and to be her 'one slave in the world', Will repeatedly assumes the posture of the courtly lover, placing his lady on a pedestal and worshipping her from afar. This distance is made necessary at the outset, of course, by the fact of Dorothea's marriage to Casaubon, but

Will's tendency to adore his lady seems perilously close to the destructive worship of Gilfil, Wakem and Tito.

As these earlier courtly lovers also reveal, a predictable outcome of Will's worship of Dorothea is her subordination to him in their marriage, described in the Finale as one in which her 'wifely help' is 'absorbed into the life of another' so that she is 'only known in a certain circle as a wife and mother'. In this relationship – a version of the marriage Dornberg had desired with Armgart, where the woman's 'possible' is 'absorbed' by the husband's 'Actual' – Dorothea is described as happy, but the narrator also dwells at some length on 'the conditions of an imperfect social state' that have kept her from pursuing her original public aims. Will, on the other hand, finds happiness in his private life while also becoming 'an ardent public man'. His son, moreover, acquires even more scope for development than his father had: in the Finale, much attention is given to the question of whether or not Brooke will cut off the entail; his decision not to do so makes Dorothea's son the heir of the Brooke estate who, when he is grown, has the freedom to decide not to represent Middlemarch in Parliament because he thinks 'that his opinions [have] less chance of being stifled if he remain[s] out of doors'. This son, in other words, has not only the freethinking tendencies of his father but also the wealth of a member of the gentry, inherited from his mother, and the masculine freedom to choose one career over another. His happy fate combines the best aspects of his parents' lives without their limitations.

The same range of opportunity and choice presumably is not available to Dorothea's second child, however, who is mentioned only in a vague reference to 'the two cousins' of 'dubiously mixed' blood who visit Celia's children at Tipton. Though this child's gender is never made explicit, the fact that the first is called 'Dorothea's son', not her 'elder son', implies that the second is a daughter. Significantly, the fate of this second and secondary child is a notable absence in the novel's Finale. Like her mother's influence, which the narrator both laments and celebrates as 'incalculably diffusive', this child is associated only with the 'unhistoric acts' that benefit the world but leave their performers in 'unvisited tombs'. The existence of this child thus emerges as one of several details that contribute to a disturbing doubleness in the novel's Finale: while presenting a happy closure to the romance plot and so fulfilling the generic expectations created by such a narrative structure, the Finale simultaneously reminds the reader of those aspirations the romance plot by definition suppresses or excludes. It is possible, in fact, that Dorothea's second child and presumed daughter is among those referred to in the Finale's darkest statement: 'But we insignificant people with our daily words and acts are preparing the lives of many Dorotheas, some of which may present a far sadder sacrifice than that of the Dorothea whose story we know.' In this conclusion to the novel's penultimate paragraph, the narrator's use of 'we' adds to self-accusation a strong charge against both the romance form itself and the patriarchal culture that demands a 'sacrifice' in some form from all of its women.

This emphasis in the Finale on 'the lives of many Dorotheas' may also be a reference back to the other women in the novel whose fates have also been interpreted in terms of the romance plot. Even Rosamond Vincy, for example, the figure from the rising middle class whose characterisation simultaneously epitomises and satirises the ideal romance heroine, unknowingly pays a price for the perverse fulfilment ascribed to her at the end of the novel. Rosamond's very destructiveness is the result of her unquestioning acceptance of her feminine fate and her similarly unreflective adherence to middle-class aspirations about rising financially and socially through marriage. From the first mention of her in the novel, when she is discussed as a sexual object by the men at the Brooke dinner-party,

Rosamond is presented as a successful player of feminine
roles who enjoys the appropriating male gaze. As a result,
even her suffering is trivial and clichéd. As the narrator
reports of the ten days during which Lydgate stays away
from the Vincy household, 'Poor Rosamond lost her appetite
and felt as forlorn as Ariadne – as a charming stage Ariadne left
behind with all her boxes full of costumes and no hope of a
coach' (31). This cynical image stands in startling contrast
to that of the desolate Dorothea standing in front of
Ariadne's statue in Rome, oppressed by the baffling sense
that neither her yearning for affection nor her desire for
masculine knowledge can be satisfied by her marriage. The
contrast points up the main difference between the two
women: that Dorothea's desires extend beyond what patriarchy has ascribed to women, while Rosamond's do not.

The Ariadne image also suggests, however, that there are
notable similarities between Dorothea and Rosamond, and
these serve often to dramatise the extent to which both of
them are able to seek fulfilment of their desires only
through marriage. Like Dorothea, therefore, Rosamond
fantasises about a married future that will correct all that is
unsatisfactory in her life, only to choose a man who will fail
to implement her plan. The first marriages of the two
women are also similar. Lydgate, of course, is presented
more sympathetically than Casaubon, but, like the older
man, he expects that his marriage will give him additional
time for his career and so looks forward to the end of
courtship. Lydgate's condescending attitute toward women
makes his choice of Rosamond a natural one: while she
seeks a man who will elevate her socially, he looks for a
woman who is 'polished, refined', and 'docile' (16). For
him, as for Casaubon, 'one of the prettiest attitudes of the
feminine mind' is 'to adore a man's pre-eminence without
too precise a knowledge of what it consist[s] in' (27). For
this reason, though Lydgate in his 'narrowed lot' (81) invites sympathy after he is defeated by Rosamond's 'studied

negation' and 'inward opposition' to him (63), it is also apparent that he is paying the price for his patriarchal view of women. Attracted to them, like Don Silva, for what he perceives to be 'the weakness of their frames and the delicate poise of their health both in body and mind' (64), he is mastered by a woman who uses her subordination as an instrument of power. The Lydgate marriage is thus a grotesque parody of the romantic ideal that requires the absorption of the woman's life in the man's. In these terms, it is significant that the references in the Finale to Rosamond's happiness with her second husband, while sardonically reported, do not include any of the qualifiers that are attached to Dorothea's fulfilment in her second marriage: for Rosamond, the romance plot imposes no limitations on her desire precisely because her desire, so perfectly in accordance with her position in patriarchy, is itself so limited.

The third major focus of the romance plot in *Middlemarch*, the marriage of Mary Garth and Fred Vincy, appears to offer a simpler, more pastoral version of the courtship narrative than the Dorothea and Rosamond stories. Mary, indeed, who represents the lower middle class, stands in radical contrast with both of the other two women. Unlike Dorothea in her first marriage, she prefers to look down on her husband and assumes a maternal rather than a daughterly relationship with him. Unlike both Dorothea and Rosamond in their first marriages, moreover, she has no illusions about how her husband will transform her life. All of Mary's decisions are presented as compromises, choices of a lesser evil: she nurses Featherstone in order to avoid being a governess; when he dies, she arranges for a position in a school in York because she is '*less unfit* to teach in a school than in a family' (40: italics added); when Fred's prospects look unpromising, she resolves to remain, in defiance of the stereotype of the old maid, 'single and merry' (86); and she finally marries Fred rather than Mr Farebrother, who can offer her 'new dignities and an acknowledged value of which she had often felt the absence', because she cannot allow any 'cheapening' of her original affection for Fred (57). The first three of these decisions are made in response to a realistic appraisal of her inferior financial and social position – in these terms, Mary's freedom is much more limited than that of Dorothea or Rosamond – but the choice of Fred over Farebrother seems merely a version of the romantic notions that led Nancy Lammeter in *Silas Marner* to reject all suitors except the less than desirable Godfrey Cass. The decision also seems to reflect Mary's need to stand in a position of authority over her husband. As she says to her father, 'husbands are an inferior class of men, who require keeping in order' (86).

In this thinking, Mary seems to be repeating the pattern of her parents' marriage, in which Caleb Garth, as Farebrother reports, 'would hardly have pulled through as he has done without his wife' (17). Interestingly, Susan Garth's devotion to her husband, while generally presented as a positive influence, is also the subject of an acutely ironic analysis by the narrator. A governess turned housewife, Susan is proud to demonstrate to her pupils, whom she trains in her kitchen, that she can be educated without living as 'a useless doll' (14). Susan's beliefs about sexual difference do not reflect, however, this repudiation of the Victorian attitude toward respectable womanhood. They express, rather, views of gender that are in their way as essentialist as those of Brooke, Chettam, Casaubon and Lydgate. As the narrator remarks, she was 'apt to be a little severe towards her own sex, which in her opinion was framed to be entirely subordinate. On the other hand, she was disproportionately indulgent towards the failings of men, and was often heard to say that these were natural' (14).

Given these views, it is not surprising that Susan Garth saves money to educate only her sons and that she should use for this purpose even Mary's hard-earned income. Another result of Susan Garth's view of men and women is the loss of the ironic voice that the youthful Mary has inherited from her:

> Not that she was inclined to sarcasm and to impulsive sallies, as Mary was. *In her present matronly age, at least,* Mrs. Garth never committed herself by over-hasty speech; having, as she said, borne the yoke in her youth, and learned self-control. She had that rare sense that discerns what is unalterable, and submits to it without murmuring. (24: italics added)

Here Susan's suppression of her ironic feminine voice is revealed to be an early response to the recognition of the futility of speaking out. The logic underlying Susan's silent resignation, moreover, while it may lead in her own case to a reasonably happy marriage, is exposed by other plots in the novel as patently self-destructive. In the case of Dorothea's marriage to Casaubon, submission 'without murmuring' is hardly an answer to her troubles, and even Mary's own marriage, modelled so closely on her mother's, requires a suppression of the woman that stands in direct opposition to the narrator's sympathetic stance on female aspiration. Farebrother's proposal is presented as a 'painful' temptation for Mary to indulge 'fleeting visions' of a better life (57), and her position with regard to Fred is then interestingly reflected in the narrator's comment, made toward the end of the novel's last chapter, that when 'he grasped her hand . . . till it rather hurt her', she 'would not complain'. Here, in a small way, Mary is seen accepting exactly the role of female suffering that the novel elsewhere radically calls into question. The happy closure of her courtship plot, achieved in part by the sacrifice of her own desires, is thus ultimately seen as dramatising its own limitations. This is most apparent in the Finale, where Mary's marriage becomes the focus for extensive ironic comment. Though she and Fred are described as achieving 'solid mutual happiness', it is seen to be based on Mary's silent devotion to Fred's career. Like her mother, it seems, she has given up even the voice of caustic comment. Thus when Fred expresses the belief 'that he [can] make money by the purchase of a horse which turns[s] out badly', Mary attributes the 'fault' to the horse, not to 'Fred's judgment'.

The irony directed at the marriage of Mary and Fred is generally mild, but the issue of how their values will be carried down into the next generation has serious implications. Mary is the mother of three sons and, the narrator comments, 'was not discontented that she brought forth men-children only'. The double negative here, however – in keeping with Mary's habit of making choices based not on positive benefits but on degrees of deprivation – emphasises her avoidance of discontent rather than any achievement of contentment. The comment is made all the more ironic, moreover, by its allusion to Shakespeare's Lady Macbeth, whose husband says these words to her after she has passionately urged him on to perform his role in the murder of Duncan: 'Bring forth men-children only! / For thy undaunted mettle should compose / Nothing but males' (1.7.73–5). Mary obviously has none of Lady Macbeth's violence, but the suggestion that bearing sons rather than daughters is a function of woman's masculine 'mettle' is disturbing, especially in light of the fact that Mary's book, written 'for her boys', is entitled 'Stories of Great Men, taken from Plutarch'. Such a book, which appeals to the ambitions of boys but not girls, seems a telling reflection of the consistent exclusion of Mary's own aspirations from her marriage. Eliot's personal notes on Plutarch, which mention 'heroic wifehood' in the Cleomenes story and allude to 'Plutarch's interpretation Concerng. the Virtues of Women', suggest all the more strongly that the presence of female subordination is a necessary condition for male greatness.[8] In their parents' marriage and in the narratives their mother writes down for them, this is the understanding of gender difference offered to Mary Garth's sons.

The same lesson is also imposed on Mary's younger siblings, Ben and Letty, who have been present in many of the Garth family scenes as representing still another version of the hierarchical sibling relationship seen in Maggie and Tom Tulliver, Lillo and Ninna of *Romola*, the children of the 'Brother and Sister' sonnets, and Dorothea's unnamed children. Ben is seen from the first time he appears as an aggressive child obsessed with power: he uses Fred's whip to torment a cat, asks Mary to make with breadcrumbs the image of a peacock, and thinks his father is like Cincinnatus, whose heroism he has learned about from his educated mother. Letty, on the other hand, has a life that is continually 'checkered by resistance to her depreciation as a girl' (57) and appears in the Finale, like Maggie, using the knowledge she has learned from books to defeat her brother's assertions about male superiority – only to be refuted by the 'oracular sentence' of a mother who prefers boys over girls.

The unmitigated frustration of Letty in the midst of the Finale's happy closure, like similar instances of discordance in the conclusions of Eliot's earlier fictions (her name echoes that of Hetty), serves not only to modify the reader's sense of satisfaction but also to draw attention to the very assumptions and ideologies that underlie the romance plot and its conventional fulfilment. Thus both the limited happiness of the three married women and the frustration of Letty are based on the necessity within patriarchy that the feminine remain subordinate. As Eliot herself said of the Finale to *Middlemarch* in a letter to Sara Hennell, 'Expect to be immensely disappointed with the close of *Middlemarch*. But look back to the Prelude' (*GEL* 5: 330).

Letty's suppression also reminds the reader of other female characters whose own sacrifice has been necessary for the fulfilment of the romance plot: Miss Morgan, the governess in the Vincy household who intermittently appears looking 'brown, dull, and resigned' (16) and who is called upon to sew Rosamond's wedding clothes; the overworked Mrs Dagley, 'a thin, worn woman, from whose life pleasure had so entirely vanished that she had not even any Sunday clothes which could give her satisfaction in preparing for church' (39); and Tantripp, whose devotion to Dorothea Brooke is strongly reminiscent of that of Denner for Mrs Transome. All of these women, like Letty, leave the reader mindful as well of Will Ladislaw's mother, who was 'at a discount' in the eyes of her parents while her brother was alive and whose mother finally pursued her because, 'having lost her boy', she 'imagined a grandson' (61). Nor are subordinate women the only characters whose sacrifices accomplish the romance closure. Camden Farebrother, like Seth Bede, is also presented in the end as deprived of his desired fulfilment precisely because he has not assumed a patriarchal role. In the world of *Middlemarch*, as in that of Eliot's earlier fictions, a failure to subscribe to prescribed gender roles results in exclusion from the narrative's happy closure. In achieving its fulfilment, the romance plot simultaneously exposes its own narrow and oppressive ideology.

The romance plot is even more directly attacked in Eliot's last novel, *Daniel Deronda*, whose lack of a Conclusion, Epilogue, or Finale signals its open-ended structure and its departure from any standard closure: here the widowed heroine is seen, not fulfilled by a second, happier marriage, as Dorothea is, or by her matriarchal position, as Romola is, but vaguely anticipating or hoping for a selfless future in which she will be 'one of the best of women, who make others glad that they were born' (70). More disturbing still is the prominent disparity – generally seen in Eliot's fiction only between central and subordinate story lines – between the 'Gwendolen Harleth' and 'Daniel Deronda' plots, both of which receive sustained narrative treatment. In this last of

Eliot's novels, as its titular privileging of a masculine name suggests, masculine desire appears to be satisfied by the patriarchal rewards of loving wife and meaningful vocation, while feminine desire – though it is given extensive space in the story – is left without even an object to be yearned for.

These radical anomalies in the ending of *Daniel Deronda* do not make the novel altogether different from the Eliot texts that preceded it, however. A striking feature of this last work is its complex reworking of relationships and situations from the earlier works, going back even to the stories in *Scenes of Clerical Life*. The position of Tina Sarti, for example, is in the later work segmented and extended into the predicaments of several characters: Deronda is like her in being adopted by a family whose title and property he cannot inherit; Lydia Glasher is like her in her position as abandoned woman and in her related association with the Medusa image; Mirah Lapidoth is like her in her role as orphaned and impoverished dark heroine; and Gwendolen Harleth is like her in her plan, never carried out, to attack her lover with a knife. Similar parallels can be seen in the situations of Janet Dempster and Gwendolen, both of whom are married to abusive husbands and turn in their misery to a man – Tryan and Deronda, respectively – for consolation and inspiration. In both these cases, the parallels between the two fictions act as a comment on the resolution of the earlier work: Tina's suffering is echoed in Gwendolen's continuing predicament, but in *Daniel Deronda* it cannot be so easily subsumed by romantic images of the lost wife. The comparison with 'Janet's Repentance' is more striking: though Gwendolen, like Janet, is finally rid of her abusive husband, the male mentor cannot be counted on to alter her life, any more than an adopted child can. The lack of resolution in Gwendolen's plot, in other words, calls into question the supposed fulfilment of earlier plots. Such comparisons can even be made in terms of minor characters: the strategy employed by the loathsome Lush in *Daniel*

Deronda of 'stint[ing] his wife and daughters of calico in order to send his male offspring to Oxford' offers a damning comment on the differently treated but analogous household economy imposed by Susan Garth in *Middlemarch*.

In other parallels between plots, the reverse is true: the earlier resolution serves to challenge a presumed moment of fulfilment in the plot of *Daniel Deronda*. Thus Mirah's seemingly successful attempt to recover the maternal body through reunion with the brother she worships is undermined by the recollection of Maggie Tulliver's unsuccessful – indeed fatal – attempt to do the same; and both Mordecai's and Daniel's roles as mentor figures (to Daniel and Gwendolen, respectively) are seriously called into question by Savonarola's oppressive influence over Romola. Deronda's fulfilment through Judaism is undermined chiefly through its similarity to Fedalma's more problematic discovery of her Gypsy roots and to the parallel between Mordecai and Zarca, another oppressive father figure. *Daniel Deronda* thus serves as a fiction that both destabilises and is destabilised by other works in the Eliot corpus: by its repetitions with radical difference, it deconstructs and is deconstructed by the resolutions in the earlier novels.

This basic indeterminacy of *Daniel Deronda* – in its relation both to itself and to other works by Eliot – is linked to the construction of desire in the novel, which is often seen in terms of an Oedipal struggle or of a yearning for the pre-Oedipal union with the maternal body. And just as the desire for the phallus which lies at the heart of the Oedipal crisis follows upon the discovery of the separateness of the mother, so desire itself is exposed in this novel as the longing for objects that can serve merely as imperfect substitutions for an original, imagined, lost object. This strategy of displacement can be seen equally in male characters and in female, in characters who know their actual mothers and in those who seek a remembered or imagined maternal figure. The novel thus psychoanalyses the standard plots of marriage, of vocation, and of quest for the lost origin, revealing the illusoriness and the interchangeability of their objects of desire. Wife, husband, vocation, nationhood, father, mother – all these conventional objects of desire are revealed to be arbitrary substitutions used to compensate for a fundamental sense of loss or lack; they are demystified and degendered.

The novel does not, however, erase altogether the cultural category of gender. Rather, it undermines essentialist definitions of gender difference by revealing the extent to which, although the sense of lack that sets desire in motion is common to female and to male subjects, the *objects* of desire constructed by patriarchal culture are gender-coded. For example, both Daniel Deronda and his mother desire a vocation, but only a male subject can with impunity seek this unattainable object. A similar comparison can be made between Gwendolen Harleth and Henleigh Grandcourt (whose initials are transpositions of each other), both of whom seek absolute control in marriage: because of her gender, Gwendolen is less able than Grandcourt to approach the position of power, illusory though it ultimately is for the man or for the woman. The novel thus dramatises both the falsity and the force of gender definitions in patriarchal culture.

This simultaneous acknowledgement and destabilising of essentialist gender difference is apparent in the sister–brother pairing of Mirah and Mordecai. Both desire an illusory lost mother (imaged in the memory of the actual mother who has died), and both fix upon Deronda as a phallic substitute to fill this perceived absence, but each assumes a different position in relation to the desired object: in her marriage, Mirah seeks to subsume her identity into Deronda's, while Mordecai attempts, through his 'marriage of . . . souls' (63) with Deronda, to inhabit the other man's identity and so to survive even beyond death. The relationship among these three characters, moreover, actually

constitutes a bond between the two men, with Mirah as
mediating object: the heterosexual 'marriage' makes possible the privileged union of Mordecai and Daniel, who in
their common Judaism see themselves as brothers who 'fed
at the breasts' of the same mother (63). This link of
brotherhood with the standard quest for the lost mother
excludes Mirah – the only person who actually did suck at
the same breasts as Mordecai – making her a vehicle rather
than an agent of desire.

Nor can Mirah find any such vehicle of her own on which
to fix her quest for the lost maternal body, figured in her
desire to hear again her mother's Hebrew: the *Semitic* song
is for Mirah an expression of what Julia Kristeva has called
the pre-Oedipal *semiotic* language. As Mirah tells Mrs
Meyrick,

> I think my life began with waking up and loving my
> mother's face: it was so near to me, and her arms were
> round me, and she sang to me. . . . They were always
> Hebrew songs she sang; and because I never knew the
> meaning of the words they seemed full of nothing but our
> love and happiness. When I lay in my bed and it was all
> white above me, she used to bend over me between me
> and the white, and sing in a sweet low voice. (20)

Mirah's preface to her comments, 'I think my life began',
signals that what follows is a conflation of memory and
fantasy, a substitution of a dead actual mother for a desired
imaginary lost unity. Thus although Deronda's own fear
that Mirah will be disappointed in finding her actual mother
is rooted in elitism and anti-Semitism, he is correct in
thinking that there is no one to match Mirah's vision of
infantile bliss, no one to intervene 'between [her] and the
white' of alienating otherness.

In Mirah's world, that otherness is embodied chiefly by
the father who took her away from her mother and who

used her voice and body as his main source of income. Lapidoth represents to Mirah denial and suppression of her desire. 'It was this way of turning off everything,' she remarks, 'that made a great wall between me and my father, and whatever I felt most I took the most care to hide from him' (20). In Mirah's mind, the possibility for return to pre-Oedipal happiness resides in finding as a substitute for the lost mother her brother Ezra, whose voice and presence she remembers in association with the maternal dyad. She describes how 'I remember my mother's voice once calling, "Ezra!" and then his answering from the distance, "Mother!"... and then he came close to us' (32). When Deronda then orchestrates the reunion of Mirah and Mordecai, it is presented as if it were a return to the lost mother:

They looked at each other, motionless. It was less their own presence that they felt than another's; they were meeting first in memories, compared with which touch was no union. Mirah was the first to break the silence, standing where she was.

'Ezra,' she said, in exactly the same tone as when she was telling of her mother's call to him.

Mordecai with a sudden movement advanced and laid his hands on her shoulders. He was the head taller, and looked down at her tenderly while he said, 'That was our mother's voice. You remember her calling me?'

'Yes, and how you answered her – "Mother!" – and I knew you loved her.' Mirah threw her arms around her brother's neck, clasped her little hands behind it, and drew down his face, kissing it with childlike lavishness. (47)

Here both Mirah and Mordecai discover the mother in each other, but this symmetry gradually disappears as Mirah – even as she speaks in the tones of the mother – assumes the position of the child. Their relationship is then established firmly in terms of gender roles, with Mordecai

as guardian and Mirah as nurse. The entrance of Deronda
into this partnership merely extends and duplicates the
same roles: Deronda reinforces his bond with Mordecai by
marrying Mirah and at Mordecai's death, through their
'marriage' of souls, becomes Mordecai's avatar – another
substitute for the lost maternal body.

Such a reading could suggest that the Mordecai-Mirah-
Daniel triad successfully substitutes for an imagined pre-
Oedipal dyad, but the plot's continuing asymmetry, enforced
by gender difference, reveals the inadequacy of such an
interpretation. Thus while Mordecai momentarily returns
to the memory of his actual mother in his reunion with
Mirah, his yearning for the imaginary lost dyad is expressed
much more intensely in his bond with Deronda, who
discovers Mordecai's identity as Mirah's brother when
Mordecai mentions his name 'Ezra'. Significantly, Mordecai
links this buried name with his actual mother and in turn
associates her with a sense, not of infantile bliss, but of
curtailed freedom.[9] The mention of his old name, he tells
Deronda, 'was like the touch of a wand that recalled me to
the body wherefrom I had been released as it were to mingle
with the ocean of human existence, free from the pressure of
individual bondage' (43). For the patriarchal Mordecai, the
primordial image of water is linked not with the mother,
but with escape from the maternal body. For him, bliss lies
not in returning to an imagined past unity but rather in
constructing a future one by impregnating – and becoming
– the soul of Deronda. In attempting to do this, Mordecai
plays, not child, but lover, mother, and father to Deronda
in a relationship that is at once erotic, 'maternal' (40), and
'half-dominat[ing]' (41). In significant ways, his paternal
role is like those of Savonarola with Romola, Casaubon with
Dorothea, and Zarca with Fedalma: Mordecai too uses the
language of silence after speech and by it seeks to extend
his influence over Deronda beyond death. The effect of
Mordecai's 'dead hand' is different from that of these

others, however, precisely because the object of his projections is a fellow male. In accepting his own Judaism and embracing his friend's cause, Deronda – rather than repressing his own desire, like the women under such paternal influences – guarantees for himself the two rewards of the male *Bildungsroman*: marriage and vocation.

The fulfilment of the Mordecai–Deronda plot is undermined, however, by its contrast with the position of the woman who acts as a 'hidden connection' (46) between them, for Mirah's relationship with both her husband and her brother, like that with her father, involves a suppression rather than an assertion of self. Her discovery of Deronda's Judaism, for example, gives her – not the extension of identity that Mordecai feels – but only 'a new timidity under [his] glance and near presence' (63). And his proposal to her – not entirely unlike that of Tito to Romola – is presented as an offer to establish a tie with her father. In these terms, it is especially significant that Lapidoth's final fate is left unresolved in the plot's conclusion: having stolen the ring of *Deronda's* father, he suggests by his absence only that he will reappear at an inopportune time: the suppressing otherness of the father has not been eliminated by the Daniel–Mirah marriage.

Nor does Mirah's relationship with Mordecai, which is based on her 'worshipping' (52) attitude toward him, constitute a satisfactory return to the mother, for it involves not a reclamation of her mother's melodic and inscrutable primordial language, but rather a silencing in the face of her brother's authoritative command of Hebrew words and their meanings – learned not from his mother but from her Rabbi brother. Duplicating his own education, Mordecai recites Hebrew verses for little Jacob Cohen with the intention of 'getting them engraved' or 'print[ed]' on the boy, who as a man will embrace their (i.e. *his*) meanings. 'My words may rule him some day,' Mordecai remarks. 'Their meaning may flash out on him. It is so with a nation –

after many days' (38). That the *meaning* of words and their relationship to nationhood is a masculine province is clear from Mordecai's and Mirah's differing positions with respect to language. In contrast to Mirah's 'usual posture of crossed hands and feet, with the effort to look as quiet as possible', stands Mordecai's 'old sense of enlargement in utterance' (63), his resolve to embody and pass down the ancient tongue of his patriarchal past. The price of Mirah's silence in the face of her brother's control of language and meaning is abundantly clear in the single moment when she challenges his authority by questioning his interpretation of the story about the Jewish maiden who loved the Gentile king. In opposition to Mordecai's insistence that the maiden possesses a characteristically female love 'that loses self in the object of love', Mirah argues for 'her strong self, wanting to conquer'. Mordecai condescendingly rejects Mirah's theory, suggesting that she has been influenced by plays she has read rather than by 'thy own heart, which is like our mother's'. That Mirah 'makes no answer' to this charge, particularly after her expression of passionate identification with the maiden, makes the meaning of her silence complex and indeterminate: the question of the nature of their mother's heart – as well as the question of the nature of Mirah's own heart – is left for the reader to ponder.

The possibility suggested by this impasse – that Mirah's 'heart' might be different from her mother's, or from the 'heart' that Mordecai imputes to their mother – relates to an issue that emerges more clearly in the novel's treatment of living mothers. While the dead mother can readily be equated with the lost dyadic union, it is difficult to identify an actual breathing woman with this imagined projection: when the 'mother' as projected 'other' is seen to be a speaking subject, she ceases to be the maternal body and becomes 'her strong self'. This fact complicates the relationship of Gwendolen Harleth with her mother Fanny Davilow, which, as Carpenter has pointed out, is based on Gwendolen's 'prideful phallic fantasy' that 'she herself is the Phallus, for she *is* what her mother desires'.[10] Gwendolen can operate under this delusion precisely because Fanny has given her eldest daughter the power of the phallic man. Like Mirah with Mordecai and Deronda, Fanny identifies her own happiness with Gwendolen's and thinks of her as a 'goddess' (44). When Gwendolen does break down, therefore, Fanny is unable to think of her as fallible and feels 'something of the alarmed anguish that women feel at the sight of over-powering sorrow in a strong man; for this child had been her ruler' (7). Gwendolen is equally incapable of compre-hending Fanny's difference, as her failure to fetch her mother's medicine makes clear. Lying 'snug and warm as a rosy infant in her little couch', Gwendolen cannot leave her womb-like bliss to 'step out in the cold' (3). For similar reasons, she strangles her sister's canary when it interrupts her singing: Gwendolen cannot tolerate interruption of pleasure, her only remaining vestige of the comfort associ-ated with the mother's body. This inability on Gwendolen's part to comprehend her mother as speaking subject exposes the fissure in the imagined maternal dyad: to be one with the mother is to deny her the self which, in the words of the narrator of *Felix Holt*, is 'larger than [her] maternity' (8).

To a limited extent, however, Gwendolen does learn by the end of the novel to differentiate herself from the mother. As Carpenter interestingly argues, the plot traces Gwen-dolen's painful break from Fanny and then goes on to con-struct 'the bond between mother and daughter as more crucial, more painful, and more meaningful than that of the daughter's "seduction" (by the Father)'.[11] This insistence on the primacy in the novel's closure of a new mother–daughter bond still privileges the daughter's needs, how-ever, and does not take fully into account the mother's separate self. Absent from the novel's ending, therefore, is a satisfactory conclusion to the situation of the Alcharisi – the woman who admitted she did not want to marry or to have children, who gave up her first child when he was only two years old, and who spoke indifferently of the offspring she bore afterwards. Her mention of 'five children' rather than 'five sons' suggests, moreover, that at least one of them is a daughter. If the Fanny–Gwendolen bond in the novel's ending confers a kind of sacredness on the mother–daughter relationship, then the problematic life of the Alcharisi serves to call this resolution into question.

The chapter which depicts Deronda's first meeting with 'the longed-for mother' is headed by a motto taken from Eliot's poem, 'Erinna', which describes the anguish of the Greek poetess at being confined to a feminine role of making linen for mummies while men engage in 'deeds' or 'song'. This image of the frustrated female artist prepares the reader for the portrayal of a woman whose 'passionate self-defence' challenges the most basic Victorian definitions of woman as wife and mother: the Alcharisi marries only for convenience (first to escape her father's power and then to hide her deteriorating talent) and tells her first child, 'I did not wish you to be born'. Her marriage to Daniel's father, in which the husband gives up his career in order to devote his life to the wife's art, is a radical inversion of the standard Victorian marriage. The Alcharisi defies as well her Jewish origin. She explains to Daniel, 'I was born amongst them without my will. I banished them as soon as I could' (53).

This response to her roots – so different from Mordecai's embrace of his origins – is linked to the Alcharisi's role as the daughter of a patriarchal father who thinks of his daughter as 'an instrument' for securing a male heir (51). Next to this biological role, her own desires are negligible:

He never comprehended me, or if he did, he only thought of fettering me into obedience. I was to be what he called 'the Jewish woman' under pain of his curse. I was to feel everything I did not feel, and believe everything I did not believe. (51)

The Alcharasi's refusal of the maternal role – as well as her insistence that Daniel be raised as a Gentile – was thus an act of defiance toward the father who failed to acknowledge her separateness from his own desire. Her passionate pursuit of her artistic career – similar in its intensity to Mordecai's and Daniel's embrace of Judaism – is thus a declaration of separateness, of the need to be defined outside the father's will. She asks Daniel,

> 'Had I not a rightful claim to be something more than a mere daughter and mother? The voice and the genius matched the face. Whatever else was wrong, acknowledge that I had a right to be an artist, though my father's will was against it. My nature gave me a charter'. (53)

This proud declaration on the Alcharisi's part stands in tension, however, with the fact that she has never actually escaped patriarchal definitions. Her impossible predicament is apparent in her desperate words to Daniel about her father's reduction of her to his image of 'the Jewish woman':

> He wished I had been a son; he cared for me as a makeshift link. His heart was set on his Judaism. He hated that Jewish women should be thought of by the Christian world as a sort of ware to make public singers and actresses of. As if we were not the more enviable for that! That is a chance of escaping from bondage. (51)

The Alcharisi reveals here – almost against her will – that the escape from one form of bondage constitutes the entrance into another: to be a Jewish woman or a Jewish actress was to be a 'ware' possessed and exchanged by men. This fact is underscored by Mirah's story, an exact reversal of the Alcharasi's: while Mirah flees the bondage of acting and singing that is imposed by her father and seeks the Judaism of her mother and brother, the Alcharisi flees the Judaism imposed by her father and seeks the career in performance made possible by the voice training given her by her dead mother's sister, aptly named Leonora (Beethoven's Leonore capably performs male roles). Both women escape being commodities in the possession of their exploitative fathers, but neither evades altogether the role as mediating object in a patriarchal sexual economy: Mirah enters a marriage in a culture that will make her 'a makeshift link' between generations of males, while the Alcharasi has entered a career that makes her a 'sort of ware' in 'the Christian world' and from which she is cast off when her marketable talent has diminished.

The fact remains, moreover, that neither Mirah nor the Alcharasi is completely successful at escaping even the actual father. The fate of Mirah's father is left indeterminate in the novel's closure, and the possibility is strong that his menacing presence will again interfere with her life. In the Alcharisi's case, the continuing influence of the actual father is made dramatically clear in her feeling that she has 'been forced to obey my dead father' by telling Daniel of his Jewish heritage and so bequeathing to him not only his father's fortune, but also his grandfather's chest of papers. 'My father is getting his way now' (51), she tells her son in her first interview with him. In the second interview, she is more emphatic, remarking, 'I have after all been the instrument my father wanted. – "I desire a grandson who shall have a true Jewish heart"' (53). Like Romola and Fedalma, the Alcharisi cannot help but fulfil the silent commands of the dead patriarch.

The power of the Jewish patriarch's 'dead hand' is apparent not only in the Alcharisi's sense of obligation to carry out his will, but also in the extent to which Daniel himself desires to live out his paternal heritage, in spite of what it has done to his mother. Daniel's encounter with the Alcharisi is depicted as a delayed Oedipal crisis, in which he for the first time is confronted by the actual mother and hence by her desire for something outside of himself:

> He had often pictured her face in his imagination as one which had a likeness to his own: he saw some of the likeness now, but amidst more striking differences. She was a remarkable-looking being. What was it that gave her son a painful sense of aloofness? – Her worn beauty had a strangeness in it as if she were not quite a human mother, but a Melusina, who had ties with some world which is independent of ours. (51)

The Melusina reference, in which the Alcharisi is compared to a fairy who on Saturdays was a serpent from the waist down and who could not marry any man who would see her when she was in this enchanted state, draws attention to the aspect of Daniel's mother that he has such difficulty in accepting or understanding: her role, not as wife or mother, but as singer and actress. In classic Oedipal style, Daniel is 'painfully silenced' by knowledge of the Alcharasi's second husband and children (51), but his chief difficulty is one that is not inscribed in Freud's scenario: this mother's separateness is manifested in her desire not for the father but for her art. 'You are not a woman,' she tells Daniel. 'You may try – but you can never imagine what it is to have a man's force of genius in you, and yet to suffer the slavery of being a girl' (51).

Ultimately, the novel offers no explicit answer to the Alcharisi's question, 'Shall you comprehend your mother – or only blame her?' (51), but Daniel's repeated interruptions of the Alcharisi's account of her life with questions about the father who had oppressed her imply that he has not fully grasped her problematic position within the Jewish patriarchal structure. His impassioned defence of his grandfather, moreover, suggests that even if he has stopped blaming his mother (a questionable assumption), he still has not comprehended her:

'The effects prepared by generations are likely to triumph
over a contrivance which would bend them all to the
satisfaction of self. Your will was strong, but my grandfather's trust which you accepted and did not fulfil – what
you call his yoke – is the expression of something
stronger, with deeper, farther-spreading roots, knit into
the foundations of sacredness for all men. You renounce
me – you still banish me – as a son' – there was an
involuntary movement of indignation in Deronda's voice
– 'But that stronger Something has determined that I
shall be all the more the grandson whom also you willed
to annihilate.' (53)

Here Daniel asserts his grandfather's phallic privilege over
his mother's need for 'satisfaction of self' and identifies
himself with the same 'stronger Something' that has made
women for so many 'generations' the 'makeshift link' in
patriarchal families. This commitment, moreover – as is
suggested by the narrator's reference to Daniel's indignant
voice – is presented at least partly as a response to the
discovery of the separateness of the mother. Finding
alienating difference in the maternal body for which he had
so long yearned, Daniel turns to 'his quivering imaginative
sense of close relation to the grandfather' (55). As it had for
Mordecai, the phallus replaces Deronda's lost imaginary
dyadic unity.

Daniel's failure fully to comprehend his mother's own
desire is apparent not only in his two interviews with her,
but also in his subsequent behaviour. After the Alcharasi's
account of her demeaning relationship with her father, it is
shocking to learn that Daniel is delighted by the death of
Grandcourt because he imagines 'Sir Hugo's pleasure in
being now master of his estates, able to leave them to his
daughters, or at least – according to a view of inheritance
which had just been strongly impressed on Deronda's
imagination – to take makeshift offspring as intermediate to

a satisfactory heir in a grandson' (59). Here the reference to daughters as 'makeshift offspring' in an 'intermediate' role recalls the Alcharasi's embittered description of herself as a 'makeshift link' in her father's plan for his own patriarchal succession. Combined with Daniel's readiness to think of his mother's actions as a 'breach of trust', this callous acceptance of a system of inheritance which excludes women from any role except that of providing a 'satisfactory heir' exposes his unquestioning adherence to the patriarchal system. In listening to his mother, Daniel has learned to comprehend only her father's point of view. His sense of his own past is from this point fixated on his masculine antecedents.

Daniel's response to his meeting with Kalonymos, during which he receives the chest and documents that had belonged to his grandfather, dramatises the renewal of his allegiance, which had initially been inspired by Mordecai, to the phallus:

> The moment wrought strongly on Deronda's imaginative susceptibility: in the presence of one linked still in zealous friendship with the grandfather whose hope had yearned toward him when he was unborn, and who though dead was yet to speak with him in those written memorials which, says Milton, 'contain a potency of life in them to be as active as that soul whose progeny they are', he seemed to himself to be touching the electric chain of his own ancestry; and he bore the scrutinising look of Kalonymos with a delighted awe, something like what one feels in the solemn commemoration of acts done long ago but still telling markedly on the life to-day. (60)

Here Daniel views the mystical 'electric chain of his own ancestry' as reaching back only to his male antecedents; his embrace of Judaism, reinforced by his spiritual marriage with Mordecai, constitutes the act of officially laying claim to an exclusively patriarchal line of succession.

Because these scenes take place not long before Deronda offers his final advice to Gwendolen that she 'be among the best of women, such as make others glad that they were born', its effect is to call Gwendolen's future into serious question, not to give it a sublime meaning like that bestowed upon Deronda by the discovery of his ancestral past. In these terms, Gwendolen's immediate response to Deronda's admonition reflects a more accurate reading of her own dilemma than Deronda is capable of realising: she finds his words to be 'like the touch of a miraculous hand' giving 'a strength that seemed the beginning of a new existence', but senses also that 'the new existence seemed inseparable from Deronda' (65). Alone in a patriarchal system that makes women only a reproductive 'instrument', Gwendolen without Deronda sees herself as having no place, no mission. The image of 'the electric chain' of Deronda's male ancestry – a line of succession from which Gwendolen is excluded unless she can become a mere 'makeshift link' – recalls the words of Eliot's narrator in her first short story: 'A loving woman's world lies within the four walls of her own home; and it is only through her husband that she is in any electric communication with the world beyond.' Deprived of any 'electric communication' with the 'electric chain' that links men with each other and with the public world, Gwendolen is left, like Patty Barton and the long list of self-sacrificing women who succeed her in Eliot's fiction, with no vocation except to sustain the patriarchal system that has exacted her self-effacement. That Gwendolen has, like the Alcharasi, so passionately resisted this fate makes the ending of *Daniel Deronda* the most extreme example in Eliot's corpus of a closure accomplished by a collision of the patriarchal and gender plots. From the beginning to the end of Eliot's fiction-writing career, the apparent resolutions of her novels finally expose the privileging by patriarchy of the masculine and its negation of woman's desire.

Notes

Note on Texts

Quotations are taken from the Cabinet Edition of George Eliot's works (Edinburgh, Blackwood, 1878–80). To aid readers using other editions, I have cited in parentheses chapter numbers rather than page notations. The following abbreviations also appear parenthetically with page references:

Century Gordon S. Haight (ed.) *A Century of George Eliot Criticism* (London, Methuen, 1986)

GE Gordon S. Haight, *George Eliot: A Biography* (Oxford, Oxford University Press, 1968; Harmondsworth, Penguin, 1985)

GEL Gordon S. Haight (ed.) *The George Eliot Letters*, nine vols (New Haven, Conn., Yale University Press, 1954–6, 1978)

Heritage David Carroll (ed.) *George Eliot: The Critical Heritage* (London, Routledge, 1971)

Notes to Chapter 1

1. Charles Warren Stoddard, 'George Eliot', *Exits and Entrances: A Book of Essays and Sketches* (Boston, Mass., Lathrop, 1903) pp. 143–4.

2. Quoted in George Willis Cooke, *George Eliot: A Critical Study of Her Life, Writings and Philosophy* (Boston, Mass., Osgood, 1883) p. 84.

3. Hallam Tennyson, *Alfred Lord Tennyson: A Memoir by His Son* (London, Macmillan, 1897) p. 107; Charles Eliot Norton, *Letters of Charles Eliot Norton with Biographical Comment*, 2 vols, ed. Sara Norton and M.A. DeWolfe (London, Constable, 1913) vol. 1, p. 318; Humphry House, 'Qualities of George Eliot's Unbelief', *All in Due Time: The Collected Essays and Broadcast Talks of Humphry House* (London, Hart-Davis, 1955) p. 109.

4. Joseph Jacobs, *George Eliot, Matthew Arnold, Browning, Newman: Essays and Reviews from the 'Athenaeum'* (London, Nutt, 1891) p. xvi; Cooke, pp. 81–2, 84.

5. Quoted in David Duncan, *The Life and Letters of Herbert Spencer* (1908; London, Williams, 1911) p. 296.

6. Frederic Harrison, 'George Eliot', *Studies in Early Victorian Literature*, 2nd edn (London, Arnold, 1895) pp. 231–2.

7. *Letters of Bret Harte*, ed. Geoffrey Bret Harte (Boston, Mass., Houghton, 1926) p. 163.

8. Elaine Showalter, 'Women Writers and the Double Standard', *Women*

in Sexist Society, ed. Vivian Gornick and Barbara K. Moran (New York, Basic, 1971) p. 329.

9. *Henry James Letters*, 4 vols, ed. Leon Edel (Cambridge, Mass., Harvard University Press, 1974) vol. 1, pp. 116–17.

10. Elaine Showalter, 'The Greening of Sister George', *Nineteenth-Century Fiction* 35 (1980): 292–311.

11. Quoted in Edmund Gosse, *The Life of Algernon Charles Swinburne* (New York, Macmillan, 1917) p. 236.

12. William Barry, *Heralds of Revolt: Studies in Modern Literature and Dogma* (London, Hodder, 1904) p. 12.

13. Edmund Gosse, *English Literature: An Illustrated Record*, 4 vols (London, Heinemann, 1906) vol. 4, p. 314; and 'George Eliot', *London Mercury* 1.1 (Nov. 1919): 34.

14. Mary Jacobus, *Reading Woman: Essays in Feminist Criticism* (London, Methuen, 1986) pp. 115, 203.

15. Quoted in Frances Wentworth Knickerbocker, *John Morley and His Friends* (Cambridge, Mass., Harvard University Press, 1943) p. 204.

16. Leslie Stephen, *George Eliot* (London, Macmillan, 1902) p. 155.

17. Edmond Scherer, 'George Eliot', *Essays on English Literature*, trans. George Saintsbury (London, Sampson Low, 1891) p. 270.

18. *The Letters of Robert Louis Stevenson to His Family and Friends*, 2 vols, ed. Sidney Colvin (New York, Scribner's, 1902) vol. 1, p. 141.

19. Stephen, pp. 104, 139–40.

20. F.E. Baily, *Six Great Victorian Novelists* (London, MacDonald, 1947) pp. 119, 128, 113; Margaret Crompton, *George Eliot: The Woman* (London, Cassell, 1960) p. 179; Walter Allen, *George Eliot* (New York, Macmillan, 1964) p. 48; U.C. Knoepflmacher, *Religious Humanism and the Victorian Novel: George Eliot, Walter Pater, and Samuel Butler* (Princeton, NJ, Princeton University Press, 1965) p. 12.

21. Carolyn Heilbrun praises Haight for 'refraining from masculine interpretation' in his biography (*Towards a Recognition of Androgyny* [New York, Knopf, 1973] p. 183, n. 34).

22. Gordon S. Haight, *George Eliot and John Chapman, with Chapman's Diaries* (New Haven, Conn., Yale University Press, 1940) p. vii.

23. See Haight, *George Eliot and John Chapman*, pp. 10–11, 31, 80; *GE* pp. 90, 117, 530.

24. Neil Roberts, *George Eliot: Her Beliefs and Her Art* (London, Elek, 1975) p. 97; Joseph Wiesenfarth, *George Eliot's Mythmaking* (Heidelberg, Winter, 1977) p. 29; Kathleen Adams, *Those of Us Who Loved Her: The Men in George Eliot's Life* (Warwick, George Eliot Fellowship, 1980) p. 184; Sandra Gilbert and Susan Gubar, *The Madwoman in the Attic: The Woman Writer and the Nineteenth-Century Literary Imagination* (New Haven,

Conn., Yale University Press, 1979) p. 467; John Purkis, *A Preface to George Eliot* (London, Longman, 1985) p. 37. Only Phyllis Rose (*Parallel Lives: Five Victorian Marriages* [New York, Knopf, 1983] p. 300, n. 26) and Elizabeth Ermarth (*George Eliot* [Boston, Mass., Twayne, 1985] p. 6) have even briefly criticised Haight's use of Bray.

25. Charles Bray, *Phrases of Opinion and Experience during a Long Life: An Autobiography* (London, Longman, [1885]) pp. 74–5.

26. Bray, p. 73. See also T.R. Wright, 'From Bumps to Morals: The Phrenological Background to George Eliot's Moral Framework', *Review of English Studies* 33 (1982): 37, for references to Eliot's 'facetious' letters about phrenology. For some of Eliot's taunting letters to Bray about his views on women, see *GEL* 2: 21–2, 396.

27. Luce Irigaray, *This Sex Which Is Not One*, trans. Catherine Porter with Catherine Burke (Ithaca, NY, Cornell University Press, 1985) pp. 171–2, 185–7.

28. N.N. Feltes, 'One Round of a Long Ladder: Gender, Profession and the Production of *Middlemarch*', *English Studies in Canada* 12 (1986): 216.

Notes to Chapter 2

1. For the letters see 'George Eliot', *Century Magazine* 23 (1881): 57; *GEL* 2: 438; 6: 113. See also 'School Notebook, 1834', MS N. 13, Beinecke Rare Book Library.

2. Karen Mann, *The Language that Makes George Eliot's Fiction* (Baltimore, Md, Johns Hopkins University Press, 1983) pp. 192–3.

3. John Cross, *George Eliot's Life as Related in Her Letters and Journals* (1885; Edinburgh, Blackwood, 1887) p. 17.

4. Cross, p. 40.

5. Hilary Fraser, *Beauty and Belief: Aesthetics and Religion in Victorian Literature* (Cambridge, Cambridge University Press, 1986) p. 168.

6. Nina Auerbach, *Woman and the Demon: The Life of a Victorian Myth* (Cambridge, Mass., Harvard University Press, 1982) p. 118.

7. Jacobus, *Reading Woman*, p. 107.

8. Haight, *George Eliot and John Chapman*, pp. 142–3.

9. Haight, *George Eliot and John Chapman*, p. 158.

10. Haight, *George Eliot and John Chapman*, p. 114.

11. Ruby Redinger, *George Eliot: The Emergent Self* (New York, Knopf, 1975) pp. 201, 199.

12. Rosalind Wade, 'George Eliot's Wedding', *Contemporary Review* 236 (1980): 266–7.

13. Norton, 1: 316.

14. Richard Ellmann, 'Dorothea's Husbands', *Golden Codgers: Biographical Speculations* (London, Oxford University Press, 1973) p. 30.

15. Haight, Introd. to K.A. McKenzie, *Edith Simcox and George Eliot* (London, Oxford University Press, 1961) p. xvi.

16. George Eliot, 'Art and Belles Lettres', *Westminster Review* 65 (1856): 643; 'Love in the Drama', *A Writer's Notebook 1854–1879 and Uncollected Writings*, ed. Joseph Wiesenfarth (Charlottesville, Va, University Press of Virginia, 1981) p. 255; 'The Shaving of Shagpat', *A Writer's Notebook*, pp. 265–6; 'Menander and Greek Comedy', *A Writer's Notebook*, p. 251; 'Mary Wollstonecraft and Margaret Fuller', *Essays of George Eliot*, ed. Thomas Pinney (London, Routledge, 1963) pp. 201, 205; Rev. of *Dred* by Harriet Beecher Stowe, *Essays of George Eliot*, p. 334; 'Woman in France: Madame de Sable', *Essays of George Eliot*, p. 65.

17. Gillian Beer, *George Eliot* (Bloomington, Ind., Indiana University Press, 1986) p. 40.

18. Quoted in Cross, p. 87.

19. Sandra M. Gilbert, 'Life's Empty Pack: Notes toward a Literary Daughteronomy', *Critical Inquiry* 11 (1985): 380–1, n. 22; Jennifer Uglow, *George Eliot* (London, Virago, 1987), p. 56.

20. Uglow, p. 84; Patricia Thomson, *George Sand and the Victorians: Her Influence and Reputation in Nineteenth-Century England* (London, Macmillan, 1977) p. 158.

21. Alexander Welsh, *George Eliot and Blackmail* (Cambridge, Mass., Harvard University Press, 1985) p. 116; Elaine Showalter, *A Literature of Their Own: British Women Novelists from Brontë to Lessing* (Princeton, NJ, Princeton University Press, 1977) p. 58; Jacobus, pp. 251–2.

22. Quoted in Heilbrun, pp. 73–4.

23. *Eclectic Review* 109 (Mar. 1859): 332; 'Our Weekly Gossip', *Athenaeum* (1859): 20; Rev. of *Adam Bede*, *Examiner* (Mar. 1859): 149; 'Eliot's Novels', *Quarterly Review* (1860): 498.

24. Henry Crabb Robinson, *Henry Crabb Robinson on Books and Their Writers*, ed. Edith J. Morley, 3 vols (London, Dent, 1938) 2: 787.

25. Beer, p. 23.

26. Showalter, 'The Greening of Sister George', p. 293.

27. Cross, p. 577.

28. Stoddard, pp. 146–7.

29. Beer, p. 26.

30. Georgiana Burne-Jones, *Memorials of Edward Burne-Jones*, 2 vols (New York, Macmillan, 1904) vol. 2, p. 104.

31. Quoted in Purkis, p. 76. Obsessed by the respectability of the patriarchal family name, Fanny Houghton also found it shameful that 'Mary Ann Evans' had appeared in Lewes's will (*GE*, p. 523, n. 1).

32. Irigaray, p. 173.

33. Deirdre David, *Intellectual Women and Victorian Patriarchy* (Ithaca, NY, Cornell University Press, 1987) p. x.

Notes to Chapter 3

1. Mary Poovey, *The Proper Lady and the Woman Writer: Ideology as Style in the Works of Mary Wollstonecraft, Mary Shelley, and Jane Austen* (Chicago, University of Chicago Press, 1984) p. xiv.

2. Rachel Blau DuPlessis, *Writing Beyond the Ending: Narrative Strategies of Twentieth-Century Women Writers* (Bloomington, Ind., Indiana University Press, 1985) p. 3.

3. Irigaray, p. 76.

4. Stephen Marcus, 'Eliot and Nineteenth-Century Systems of Explanation', *Salmagundi* 28 (1975): 41.

5. U.C. Knoepflmacher, 'George Eliot's Anti-Romantic Romance: "Mr Gilfil's Love-Story"', *Victorian Newsletter* 31 (1967): 14.

6. Thomas A. Noble, *George Eliot's 'Scenes of Clerical Life'* (New Haven, Conn., Yale University Press, 1968) p. 86, n. 9.

7. David Carroll, '"Janet's Repentance" and the Myth of the Organic', *Nineteenth Century Fiction* 35 (1980): 338, 348.

8. Hugh Witemeyer, *George Eliot and the Visual Arts* (New Haven, Conn., Yale University Press, 1979) p. 130; William Myers, *The Technique of George Eliot* (Leicester, Leicester University Press, 1984) p. 105.

9. Lori Hope Lefkovitz, *The Character of Beauty in the Victorian Novel* (Ann Arbor, Mich., UMI Research Press, 1987) p. 168.

10. Quoted and translated in Joseph Wiesenfarth, 'George Eliot's Notes for *Adam Bede*', *Nineteenth Century Fiction* 32 (1977): 148.

11. A close connection between Hetty and Totty is established not only by the similarity in sound of their names, but also in Totty's infantile version of her cousin's vanity. It is significant, therefore, that long before taking Hetty's pink handkerchief and seducing her, Arthur Donnithorne is seen suggestively pouring money in the 'tiny pink pocket' under Totty's frock (7).

12. Mason Harris, 'Infanticide and Respectability: Hetty Sorrel as Abandoned Child in *Adam Bede*', *English Studies in Canada* 9 (1983): 184.

Notes to Chapter 4

1. In this context it is worth noting, as Jacobus has pointed out (180–1), that Freud thought Dora's brother served her as a mediator between her and the maternal body.

2. N. Katherine Hayles, 'Anger in Different Voices: Carol Gilligan and *The Mill on the Floss*', *Signs* 12 (1986): 36–8.

3. See Elizabeth Weed, '*The Mill on the Floss* or the Liquidation of Maggie Tulliver', *Genre* 11 (1978): 444, who also views the Samuel reference as evidence of another exclusion of Maggie from patriarchy.

4. See also Beer, pp. 78–9, for a discussion of 'The Lifted Veil' as Eliot's 'vengeance on the male narrator'. The term 'one-sided knowing' was used by Lewes to describe Latimer's perspective (*GEL* 9: 220). For a discussion of the story's challenge to realistic fiction, see Terry Eagleton, 'Power and Knowledge in "The Lifted Veil"', *Literature and History* 9 (1983): 58.

5. Lawrence Jay Dessner ('The Autobiographical Matrix of *Silas Marner*', *Studies in the Novel* 11 [1979]: 269) has also compared the references to the David–Jonathan relationship in *Mill*, 'Brother Jacob', and *Silas Marner*.

6. Philip Fisher, *Making Up Society: The Novels of George Eliot* (Pittsburgh, Pa, Pittsburgh University Press, 1981) p. 109, makes a similar comparison between Godfrey and Hetty.

Notes to Chapter 5

1. The allusion to 'man's moral history' is taken from Felicia Bonaparte, *The Triptych and the Cross: The Central Myths of George Eliot's Imagination* (New York, New York University Press, 1979) p. 72. The reference to '"continuous historical" apocalypse' is taken from May Wilson Carpenter, *George Eliot and the Landscape of Time: Narrative Form and Protestant Apocalyptic History* (Chapel Hill, NC, University of North Carolina Press, 1986) p. 61.

2. F.R. Leavis, *The Great Tradition: George Eliot, Henry James, Joseph Conrad* (New York: New York University Press, 1963) p. 49.

3. Boccaccio, *The Decameron*, trans. Richard Aldington (Garden City, NY, Garden City Books, 1949) p. 255.

4. I am grateful for this perception to my colleague, Professor Elizabeth D. Harvey.

5. Margaret Homans, *Bearing the Word: Language and Female Experience in Nineteenth-Century Women's Writing* (Chicago, University of Chicago Press, 1986) pp. 206–7.

6. George Eliot, 'Margaret Fuller and Mary Wollstonecraft', *Leader* 6 (13 Oct. 1855): 988–9; rpt *Essays of George Eliot*, ed. Thomas Pinney (London, Routledge, 1963) p. 205.

7. George Eliot, *A Writer's Notebook 1854–1879 and Uncollected Writings*, ed. Joseph Wiesenfarth (Charlottesville, Va, University Press of Virginia, 1981) p. 56.

Notes to Chapter 6

1. On this reversal of Wordsworthian assumptions, see Carpenter, *George Eliot and the Landscape of Time*, pp. 179–80.

2. Carpenter, *George Eliot and the Landscape of Time*, p. 159.

3. On the Darwinian language of the Prelude and its relationship to the 'woman's nature' debate, see Beer, pp. 159–60.

4. Critics are divided about the gender of the narrator in *Middlemarch*. In my view, what is significant about this speaker is that, just as the narrative itself exposes the arbitrariness of gender categories, so s/he moves in and out of various feminine and masculine voices.

5. This connection with the early fiction is even more striking when one considers that the 'Miss Brooke' section of *Middlemarch* was originally conceived as a fourth story in *Scenes of Clerical Life*.

6. Some critics have assumed that Casaubon is impotent. The narrative is never explicit on this issue, however, a fact which forces the reader to speculate about an equally horrifying possibility: the idea of an unaffectionate Casaubon engaging in a sexual relationship with Dorothea is at least as chilling as the notion that he is impotent with her.

7. Gilbert and Gubar, pp. 528–9.

8. *Some George Eliot Notebooks*, pp. 161, 274 n. 3.

9. The differences between Mirah's and Mordecai's attitudes to the pre-Oedipal dyad are interestingly similar to Kaja Silverman's description of the two possible responses – 'charged with either intensely positive or intensely negative affect' – to the maternal voice as a 'sonorous envelope' (*The Acoustic Mirror* [Bloomington, Ind., Indiana University Press, 1988] p. 72).

10. Carpenter, '"A Bit of Her Flesh": Circumcision and "The Signification of the Phallus" in *Daniel Deronda*', *Genders* 1 (1988): 7.

11. Carpenter, '"A Bit of Her Flesh"', p. 3.

Selected Bibliography

Adams, Ian (ed.) *This Particular Web: Essays on Middlemarch* (Toronto, University of Toronto Press, 1975).

Ashton, Rosemary, *George Eliot* (Oxford, Oxford University Press, 1983).

Auerbach, Nina, *Woman and the Demon: The Life of a Victorian Myth* (Cambridge, Mass., Harvard University Press, 1982).

Austen, Zelda, 'Why Feminist Critics Are Angry with George Eliot', *College English* 37 (1976): 549–61.

Auster, Henry, *Local Habitations: Regionalism in the Early Novels of George Eliot* (Cambridge, Mass., Harvard University Press, 1970).

Beer, Gillian, 'Beyond Determinism: George Eliot and Virginia Woolf', in *Women Writing and Writing about Women*, ed. Mary Jacobus (London, Croom Helm, 1979).

—— *Darwin's Plots: Evolutionary Narrative in Darwin, George Eliot, and Nineteenth-Century Fiction* (London, Routledge, 1983; rpt London, Arc, 1985).

—— *George Eliot* (Bloomington, Ind., Indiana University Press, 1986).

Belsey, Catherine, 'Re-Reading the Great Tradition', in *Re-Reading English*, ed. Peter Widdowson (London, Methuen, 1982).

Blake, Kathleen, '*Armgart* – George Eliot on the Woman Artist', *Victorian Poetry* 18 (1980): 75–80.

—— '*Middlemarch* and the Woman Question', *Nineteenth Century Fiction* 31 (1976): 285–312.

Blind, Mathilde, *George Eliot* (London, Allen, 1883).

Bonaparte, Felicia, *The Triptych and the Cross: The Central Myths of George Eliot's Imagination* (New York, New York University Press, 1979).

Browning, Oscar, *George Eliot* (London, Walter Scott, 1890).

Brownstein, Rachel M., *Becoming a Heroine: Reading about Women in Novels* (1982; Harmondsworth, Penguin, 1984).

Carlisle, Janice, *The Sense of an Audience: Dickens, Thackeray, and George Eliot at Mid-Century* (Brighton, Harvester, 1982).

Carpenter, Mary Wilson, '"A Bit of Her Flesh": Circumcision and "The Signification of the Phallus" in *Daniel Deronda*', *Genders* 1 (1988): 1–23.

Carpenter, Mary Wilson, *George Eliot and the Landscape of Time: Narrative Form and Protestant Apocalyptic History* (Chapel Hill, NC, University of North Carolina Press, 1986).

Carroll, David (ed.) *George Eliot: The Critical Heritage* (London, Routledge, 1971).

Chase, Cynthia, 'The Decomposition of the Elephants: Double-Reading *Daniel Deronda*', *PMLA* 93 (1978): 215–27.

Chase, Karen, *Eros and Psyche: The Representation of Personality in Charlotte Brontë, Charles Dickens and George Eliot* (London, Methuen, 1984).

Christ, Carol, 'Aggression and Providential Death in George Eliot's Fiction', *Novel* 9 (1976): 130–40.

Cohen, Susan R., '"A History and a Metamorphosis": Continuity and Discontinuity in *Silas Marner*', *Texas Studies in Literature and Language* 25 (1983): 410–26.

Coslett, Tess, *Woman to Woman: Female Friendship in Victorian Fiction* (Brighton, Harvester, 1988).

Cross, J.W., *George Eliot's Life as Related in her Letters and Journals*, 3 vols (Edinburgh, Blackwood, 1885).

David, Deirdre, *Fictions of Resolution in Three Victorian Novels: North and South, Our Mutual Friend, Daniel Deronda* (New York, Columbia University Press, 1981).

—— *Intellectual Women and Victorian Patriarchy: Harriet Martineau, Elizabeth Barrett Browning, George Eliot* (Ithaca, NY, Cornell University Press, 1987).

Davidson, Cathy N. and Broner, E.M. (eds) *The Lost Tradition: Mothers and Daughters in Literature* (New York, Ungar, 1980).

Dentith, Simon, *George Eliot* (Brighton, Harvester, 1986).

Eagleton, Terry, 'Power and Knowledge in "The Lifted Veil"', *Literature and History* 9 (1983): 52–61.

Edwards, Lee R., 'Women, Energy and *Middlemarch*', *Massachusetts Review* 13 (1972): 223–38.

Edwards, Michael, 'George Eliot and Negative Form', *Critical Quarterly* 17 (1975): 171–9.

Ermarth, Elizabeth, *George Eliot* (Boston, Mass., Twayne, 1985).

Feltes, N.N., 'One Round of a Long Ladder: Gender, Profession and the Production of *Middlemarch*', *English Studies in Canada* 12 (1986): 210–28.

Fisher, Philip, *Making Up Society: The Novels of George Eliot* (Pittsburgh, Pa., Pittsburgh University Press, 1981).

Foster, Shirley, *Victorian Women's Fiction: Marriage, Freedom and the Individual* (Beckenham, Croom Helm, 1985).

Gilbert, Sandra M., 'Life's Empty Pack: Notes toward a Literary Daughteronomy', *Critical Inquiry* 11 (1985): 355–84.

Gilbert, Sandra and Gubar, Susan, *The Madwoman in the Attic: The Woman Writer and the Nineteenth-Century Literary Imagination*, New Haven, Conn., Yale University Press, 1979.

Gilligan, Carol, *In a Different Voice: Psychological Theory and Women's Development*, Cambridge, Mass., Harvard University Press, 1982.

Goode, John, '"The Affections Clad with Knowledge": Woman's Duty and the Public Life', *Literature and History* 9 (1983): 38–51.

Goodman, Charlotte, 'The Lost Brother, The Twin: Women Novelists and the Male-Female Double *Bildungsroman*', *Novel* 19 (1983): 28–43.

Gordon, Jan, 'Origins, *Middlemarch*, Endings: George Eliot's Crisis of the Antecedent', in *George Eliot: Centenary Essays and an Unpublished Fragment*, ed. Anne Smith (Totowa, NJ, Barnes, 1980).

Greenstein, Susan M., 'The Question of Vocation: From *Romola* to *Middlemarch*', *Nineteenth Century Fiction* 35 (1981): 487–505.

Gubar, Susan, '"The Blank Page" and the Issues of Female Creativity', in *Writing and Sexual Difference*, ed. Elizabeth Abel (Chicago, University of Chicago Press, 1982).

Haight, Gordon S. (ed.) *A Century of George Eliot Criticism* (London, Methuen, 1986).

—— *George Eliot: A Biography* (Oxford, Oxford University Press 1968; rpt Harmondsworth, Penguin, 1985).

—— *George Eliot and John Chapman* (New Haven, Conn., Yale University Press, 1940).

—— (ed.) *The George Eliot Letters*, 9 vols (New Haven, Conn., Yale University Press, 1954–6, 1978).

—— and von Arsdel, Rosemary T. (eds) *George Eliot: A Centenary Tribute* (London, Macmillan, 1982).

Hardy, Barbara, *Critical Essays on George Eliot* (London, Athlone, 1970).

—— *Forms of Feeling in the Victorian Novel* (London, Methuen, 1985).

—— *The Novels of George Eliot: A Study in Form* (London, Athlone, 1950).

—— *Particularities: Readings in George Eliot* (London, Peter Owen, 1982).

Harris, Mason, 'Infanticide and Respectability: Hetty Sorrel as Abandoned Child in *Adam Bede*', *English Studies in Canada* 9 (1983): 177–96.

Hayles, N. Katherine, 'Anger in Different Voices: Carol Gilligan and *The Mill on the Floss*', *Signs* 12 (1986): 23–39.

Hirsch, Marianne, 'Fraternal Plots: Beyond Repetition', in *The Mother/Daughter Plot: Narrative, Psychoanalysis, Feminism* (Bloomington, Ind., Indiana University Press, 1989).

Homans, Margaret, *Bearing the Word: Language and Female Experience in Nineteenth-Century Women's Writing* (Chicago, University of Chicago Press, 1986).

Jacobus, Mary, *Reading Woman: Essays in Feminist Criticism* (London, Methuen, 1986).

Knoepflmacher, U.C., *George Eliot's Early Novels: The Limits of Realism* (Berkeley, Calif., University of California Press, 1968).

—— 'On Exile and Fiction: The Leweses and the Shelleys', *Mothering the Mind: Twelve Studies of Writers and Their Silent Partners*, ed. Ruth Perry and Martine Watson Brownley (New York, Holmes, 1984).

—— *Religious Humanism and the Victorian Novel* (Princeton, NJ, Princeton University Press, 1965).

—— 'Unveiling Men: Power and Masculinity in George Eliot's Fiction', in *Men by Women: Women and Literature*, ed. Janet Todd (New York, Holmes, 1981).

Lefkowitz, Lori Hope, *The Character of Beauty in the Victorian Novel* (Ann Arbor, Mich., UMI Research Press, 1987).

McGuinn, Nicholas, 'George Eliot and Mary Wollstonecraft', *The Nineteenth-Century Woman: Her Cultural and Physical World*, ed. Sara Delamont and Lorna Duffin (London, Croom Helm, 1978).

McKenzie, K.A., *Edith Simcox and George Eliot* (London, Oxford University Press, 1961).

Mann, Karen, *The Language that Makes George Eliot's Fiction* (Baltimore, Md, Johns Hopkins University Press, 1983).

Mews, Hazel, *Frail Vessels: Woman's Role in Women's Novels from Fanny Burney to George Eliot* (London, Athlone, 1969).

Midler, Marcia S., 'George Eliot's Rebels: Portraits of the Artist as a Woman', *Women's Studies: An Interdisciplinary Journal* 7 (1980): 97–108.

Miller, Jane, *Women Writing about Men* (London, Virago, 1986).

Miller, Nancy K., 'Emphasis Added: Plots and Plausibilities in Women's Fiction', *The New Feminist Criticism: Essays on Women, Literature, and Theory*, ed. Elaine Showalter (New York, Pantheon, 1985).

Millett, Kate, *Sexual Politics* (Garden City, NY, Doubleday, 1970).

Moers, Ellen, *Literary Women: The Great Writers* (Garden City, NY, Doubleday, 1976).

Myers, William, *The Teaching of George Eliot* (Leicester, Leicester University Press, 1984).

Neufeldt, Victor A., 'The Madonna and the Gypsy', *Studies in the Novel* 15 (1983): 44–54.

Newton, Judith, *Women, Power and Subversion: Social Strategies in British Fiction, 1778–1860* (Athens, Ga, University of Georgia Press, 1981).

Nystul, Nancy, '*Daniel Deronda*: A Family Romance', *Enclitic* 7 (1983): 45–53.

Paris, Bernard, *Experiments in Life: George Eliot's Quest for Values* (Detroit, Mich., Wayne State University Press, 1965).

Pinney, Thomas (ed.) *The Essays of George Eliot* (London, Routledge, 1963).

Pykett, Lyn, 'Typology and the End(s) of History in *Daniel Deronda*', *Literature and History* 9 (1983): 62–73.

Redinger, Ruby, *George Eliot: The Emergent Self* (London, Bodley Head, 1976).

Rose, Jacqueline, 'George Eliot and the Spectacle of the Woman', *Sexuality in the Field of Vision* (London, Verso, 1986).

Rose, Phyllis, *Parallel Lives: Five Victorian Marriages* (New York, Knopf, 1983).

Sadoff, Dianne F., *Monsters of Affection: Dickens, Eliot, and Brontë on Fatherhood* (Baltimore, Md, Johns Hopkins University Press, 1982).

—— 'Nature's Language: Metaphor in the Text of *Adam Bede*', *Genre* 11 (1978): 411–26.

Sedgwick, Eve Kosofsky, *Between Men: English Literature and Male Homosocial Desire* (New York, Columbia University Press, 1985).

Sheets, Robin, '*Felix Holt*: Language, the Bible, and the Problematic of Meaning', *Nineteenth Century Fiction* 37 (1982): 166.

Showalter, Elaine, 'The Greening of Sister George', *Nineteenth Century Fiction* 35 (1980): 292–311.

—— *A Literature of Their Own: British Women Novelists from Brontë to Lessing* (Princeton, NJ, Princeton University Press, 1977).

Shuttleworth, Sally, *George Eliot and Nineteenth Century Science: The Make-Believe of a Beginning* (Cambridge, Cambridge University Press, 1984).

Spacks, Patricia Meyer, *The Female Imagination: A Literary and Psychological Investigation of Women's Writing* (New York, Knopf, 1975).

Tanner, Tony, *Adultery in the Novel: Contract and Transgression* (Baltimore, Md, Johns Hopkins University Press, 1979).

Thomson, Patricia, *George Sand and the Victorians: Her Influence and Reputation in Nineteenth-Century England* (New York, Columbia, 1976).

Uglow, Jennifer, *George Eliot* (London, Virago, 1987).

Vogeler, Martha S., 'The Choir Invisible: The Poetics of Humanist Piety', *George Eliot: A Centenary Tribute*, ed. Gordon S. Haight and Rosemary T. von Arsdel (Totowa, NJ, Barnes & Noble, 1982).

Weed, Elizabeth, '*The Mill on the Floss* or the Liquidation of Maggie Tulliver', *Genre* 11 (1978): 427–44.

Wiesenfarth, Joseph, *George Eliot's Mythmaking* (Heidelberg, Winter, 1977).

Winnett, Susan, 'Coming Unstrung: Women, Men, Narrative, and Principles of Pleasure', *PMLA* 105 (1990): 505–18.

Witemeyer, Hugh, *George Eliot and the Visual Arts* (New Haven, Conn., Yale University Press, 1979).

Woolf, Virginia, *The Common Reader I* (London, Hogarth, 1925).

Zimmerman, Bonnie, '*Felix Holt* and the True Power of Womanhood', *ELH* 46 (1979): 432–51.

Index